THEOLOGY FOR A NEW WORLD

THEOLOGY
FOR A NEW
WORLD

Herbert W. Richardson

SCM PRESS LTD
LONDON

0334 01616 9

© *Herbert W. Richardson 1967*

First British edition 1968
by SCM Press Ltd
56 Bloomsbury Street London WC1

Typeset in the United States of America and
Printed in Great Britain by
Fletcher & Son Ltd
Norwich

D. E. F.

Contents

Contents

Preface

The radical theologians have introduced believers in pre-Copernican Christianity to the theology of the last generation. Bishop Robinson has told us about Bultmann and Tillich; Bishop Pike has reminded us of Harnack on the Trinity.

It has been the custom of English-speaking people to adopt last year's Teutonic *Auseinandersetzung* as this year's theological fashion. Though Liverpool and London may be "mod" in music and mini skirts, "mod" in theology has traditionally been "Made in Germany". Our own theologians introduce, of course, characteristic modifications to adapt the imported product. Macquarrie's Heidegger is filtered through language analysis and the *via media* before its large-scale distribution to parsonage and pew. This procedure is tried and true.

All this, however, is almost "once upon a time". Once upon a time, men called Luther a "modern man" because they lived in the cultural period that was shaped by his doctrine and religious experience. Once upon a time, the individual and his self-consciousness and freedom were extolled as the determining factors of the age in which men lived. But this world is passing, or has passed, away. And with its passing, so too German—indeed Protestant—hegemony in theology. That is the presupposition of this book, and that is why its constructive argument attempts to sketch out the shape of a theology for another, newer age.

Several notes characterize the essays that follow. First, I have tried to keep my thinking governed by the purpose of constructive innovation. This, rather than academic contention or the shouting of radical tautol-

[ix]

ogies, is what is needed today. That the past is not the present and cannot be the future, I agree. But it hardly seems worth contending. Rather, I am interested in what theology tomorrow might be. I want to move beyond the crisis of our time towards the new world of the future.

Second, the "model" for the chapters that follow is "research and development". The qualification of every idea in this book is not that I think it to be true, much less even useful. Rather, these essays are the trying-out of various possibilities drawn from neglected parts of the Christian tradition. They may not lead anywhere at all, much less somewhere we might wish to go. But it seems to me that a systematic effort at innovation, at the development and testing of new concepts and constructions with the goal of finding some one or few that strike the right note is the task of theology today. I have my own favorites among the themes that follow; but I have preferred to present the labors of the full day's work and allow the readers to make their own selections.

Third, as with all research and development (and quite unlike mere "brainstorming"), the intellectual explorations are carried on in a systematic way. Consequently, the conceptual systems guiding the process of analysis should not be misunderstood. They are heuristic, not metaphysical devices. They are methods for the discovery of ideas and are not intended to be the permanent forms in which such ideas will be preserved and presented. I am aware that I could have eased the reader's reading by introducing a greater variety of illustrative material. But to do so might have distracted from the schemes that are being used to generate the ideas themselves. Since my purpose in these essays is to invite the reader to join with me in the process of innovation rather than to direct him to any particular set of conclusions, I have preferred to keep the heuristic structure clearly in view, confining myself to a brief, orderly presentation of essential points. These points could be expanded and footnoted, and I have elaborated many of them in historical writings prepared concurrently with this volume. Here, however, mere maps are drawn, projects plotted.

Fourth, because the schemes developed here are heuristic, they allow the employment of many "languages" rather than one. I believe the contemporary concern with the right "language" for theology—whether it should speak a Biblical, or metaphysical, or dogmatic, or ordinary tongue—is sterile. A theologian is not an English tourist, but a Swiss innkeeper. He should learn the language of others rather than requiring them to learn his own. This means, then, that he neither require Chalcedon to speak to us in the terminology of contemporary philosophy nor require ordinary men who speak ordinary language to confess their fault in the mouthings of Heideggerian anthropology. "Tourist theologians" require all the world to speak their tongue. They travel through time, stopping only at Hilton hotels, finding all else unintelligibly barbarous. They miss the new and neglected possibilities for the future hidden away in the *communio sanctorum*, whose saints and doctors converse with us by metaphysic, myth, and metaphor. In the pages that follow, we shall be speaking with some of these strange doctors as well as with some ordinary modern men. That is, we shall speak several "languages". Only Swiss innkeepers will manage the trip.

These, then, are several curiosities about this volume. Alice led us through the looking-glass to the real world; I suggest we go through the past towards the future. It is the innovative direction.

HERBERT W. RICHARDSON

Cambridge, Massachusetts
August 18, 1967

THEOLOGY FOR A NEW WORLD

I

The Sociotechnic Age

TWO VIEWS OF THE CULTURAL CRISIS

1

Many commentators on the state of modern man argue that atheism is a fundamental characteristic of our age. They do not mean simply professed atheism; they also mean existential atheism—a general loss of any sense of the reality of God, even when this is not accompanied by an explicit profession. Such a situation explains why the slogan "God is dead" has found resonance even in Christian circles. It also accounts for the fact that many people, believers and unbelievers alike, find that religious language has lost its meaning. In this respect, the crisis in modern religion does not arise primarily from intrareligious conflict (as in the sixteenth century) nor from a conflict between religion and science (as in the nineteenth century), but arises directly from the deterioration of religion itself. Modern man, it is argued, does not believe in the reality of God.

Our purpose in this chapter will be to inquire into the meaning of the phenomenon of the pervasive cultural atheism that underlies the "death of God" movement. This "public" cultural atheism is significantly different from the "private atheism" of those individuals who choose to oppose the religious beliefs of a predominantly religious culture. For example, in Jonathan Edwards' town of Northampton there was such a private atheist: Timothy Root. Howsoever Timothy arrived at his beliefs, they were his own and not those of his town. Most persons have a bit of Timothy Root in them; they have moments of private atheism when they feel, for one reason or another, that there is no God. In these periods, an irreligious individual opposes a religious culture. In public atheism, on the other hand, an entire cultural ethos is irreligious. Hence, individuals cannot set themselves against it in a moment of private atheism (though they may oppose it by an outburst of "private religion").

The thesis of the "death of God" theologians is that the modern age is tending toward a widespread public, or cultural, atheism. This presages the imminent emergence of a fully nonreligious culture wherein man will understand the world to exist through itself alone and will no longer feel any dependence on transcendent realities. In this way *homo religiosus* will become extinct.

The proposal of the "death of God" theologians depends upon relating the idea of public atheism to an hypothesis about the character of the historical process. The hypothesis is, essentially, that men were originally religious but through an irreversible process of history are becoming irreligious. The details of this theory vary from theologian to theologian. Harvey Cox utilizes Comte's notion that history has three periods: (a) an early religious period, (b) a middle metaphysical period, and (c) a modern scientific period which is antireligious and antimetaphysical. Thomas Altizer also makes use of a nineteenth-century notion: that historical development involves a movement from (a) religious transcendence to (b) atheistic immanence. These differences in their understanding of historical development are signs that the secular theologians disagree among themselves on other issues. For example, Cox is antimetaphysical, while Altizer is explicitly metaphysical; Cox does not propose any "atheistic gospel," but Altizer's gospel is one of "Christian atheism." Cox defines the modern stage of history as scientific, while Altizer shows no particular propensity to apotheosize science and technology; rather, his prophets of the modern age are artists (Blake) and metaphysicians (Hegel). Nevertheless, in spite of many disagreements among themselves, secular theologians are in accord on this single point: that public atheism is uniquely characteristic of our age because the movement of history is against religion.[1]

[1] The "secular theologians" are all those who regard "modern man" as the norm of religious truth and meaning.

2

The historical theory of the secularists is wrong because public atheism is not an exclusively modern phenomenon. I do not deny that the atheism of the modern world is significantly different from manifestations of public atheism in the past; but it is not different in the fact that it is either atheism or public. Hence, the rather crude theory of the secular theologians must be rejected because it is not true to the facts of history.

Let us briefly note three previous periods of public atheism.

1. Western civilization itself dates from a period of radical public atheism. In the fourth and fifth centuries B.C., the religion of the Greek *polis* shattered under the crisis of belief created when Persian cosmopolitanism swept over the Mediterranean world. Western civilization, i. e., the civilization which draws upon Plato and Aristotle for its inspiration, was born in this period of public atheism—during which the Greek philosophers attempted to establish a basis for religion and morality which was truly universal.

2. Western civilization in its Christian form has also endured periods of radical public atheism. For example, in the thirteenth century the Augustinian form of Christianity was shattered by Islamic science and philosophy. This science destroyed the traditional understanding of God (and creation) by demonstrating that the world must be conceived to exist eternally. Christianity endured this attack only by admitting that it is conceivable that the world might always have existed, and that God cannot be defined simply as "Eternity." To recover from this atheistic attack and to recreate a new form of religious culture, Christianity reconceived God as more than eternal. This "more" is the fact that God is the "uncaused cause" of other eternal beings. This new definition of God as "Being Itself" (*ens necessarium per se*) was the basis of the culture of the later Middle Ages.[2]

3. Perhaps the most radical outbreak of public atheism which western civilization has endured occurred in the sixteenth century. The form of this atheism was radical skepticism, the Montaignist *Que sais-je?* This skeptical atheism threatened to overthrow not only

[2] A fuller analysis of this point will be found in the introduction to Anselm of Canterbury, *Truth, Freedom, and Evil*, J. Hopkins and H. Richardson, eds. (New York, 1967), pp. 49-54.

B

human science and religion, but even human rationality itself. Many of these skeptical themes have been renewed by contemporary existentialism.

These three examples are sufficient to show that the phenomenon of public atheism is not limited to the modern world. Rather, it has existed at certain definite periods in the past. This means that the emergence of public atheism in the modern world cannot be explained as the mere *terminus* of an historical process that is tending toward an ultimate irreligion. Such an explanation stands in flat contradiction to the facts. It is ironic that the secular theologians, who talk constantly about the historical nature of man, should propose a theory of history that results from their ideological commitments rather than from a study of history itself.

3

The recurrence of public atheism at various periods in history not only contradicts the thesis that history is a process toward irreligion, but also suggests an alternative explanation of the origin and meaning of atheism. Periods of public atheism are periods of transition, marking the end of one cultural epoch and the beginning of another. The public atheism that marked the breakdown of Greek religion also marked the beginning of cosmopolitan Hellenism and the rise of universalistic Greek philosophy. The Islamic Averroism that marked the end of Augustinianism also marked the beginning of a Christian Aristotelianism (Thomism) which ascribed independence to the order of nature and also established a hierarchical basis for new patterns of authority. The skepticism that marked the end of Christian Aristotelianism also marked the beginning of a Christian individualism that acknowledged the primacy of self-consciousness and conscience and gave rise to democracy and capitalism. In each of these cases, the period of public atheism did not sustain itself, but marked a transition to another cultural epoch which was organized under a new conception of God.

The implication of these considerations for the problem of modern atheism reveals another point at which secular theologians misunderstand the present situation. They are wrong not because they claim too much for modern atheism, but because they claim too little. They argue that modern atheism is the result of modern science, modern philosophy, modern politics, and so forth. They claim that we must now undertake a criticism of traditional religion in order to bring it into line with the modern scientific world view. They argue that since we have become modern in all other respects, we should now become modern about religion. But if my argument about public atheism is correct, then the secular theologians are wrong. For they assume that religion is the last thing a given culture gets around to criticizing, whereas we have seen it is the first thing. For this reason, I argue that modern atheism is not the culmination, or perfection, of the modern world, but a sign that the modern period of history is coming to an end. This interpretation of the meaning of modern atheism is exactly contrary to the view of the secularists.

4

Atheism is not only a transitional phenomenon that signifies the end of a given cultural epoch; it is also a critical movement that possesses within itself the power to destroy a culture. The opponents of the religion of the Greek *polis* hastened its demise. The Averroists not only testified to the inadequacies of Augustinian Christianity, but by their criticism overthrew it. The humanist skeptics of the sixteenth century destroyed the assumed hierarchies and patterns of authority which were the basis of late medieval culture. Public atheism is therefore a form of radical criticism which truly marks a moment of historical transition because it also brings it about.

Moreover, not only is atheism a power of criticism; it is also its principle. The beginning of all criticism is the criticism of religion. This proposition can be validated both philosophically and historically. Cultures are established on certain assumptions, myths, and conceptions of reality for which an ultimacy, or sanctity, is claimed. Such myths maintain a culture's authority structure. Radical criticism of a given culture (i. e., the kind of criticism which results in its disintegration) must overthrow these holy ultimates. For until they are overthrown, not only will other aspects of the culture not come under radical criticism, but their questionable character will not even be recognized. It is for this reason that the beginning of all true criticism is the criticism of religion, that is, of "holy ultimates" and "sacred myths." And because public atheism is this kind of criticism of religion, it is also the beginning of all other criticism.

Atheism is the beginning of all criticism because the rejection of God (under a more or less explicit definition of that name) implies the rejection of the entire matrix of meaning which is dependent upon this holy ultimate. This matrix of meaning might be called an "intellectus" (plural: intellectus). I am suggesting that we coin this new term because such expressions as "world view" or *Weltanschauung* seem to prejudice the philosophical problem. "World view" suggests a subject-object split and a systematically unified view of things. But recent historical and philosophical studies have made us aware of the complex, unsystematic, pluralistic character of that matrix of meaning which is the felt basis for our discourse, not only about what is true and good but even about what is real. An intellectus is rooted not in thought, but in feeling; and feeling determines the kinds of things about which we want to know the truth, the kinds of things that strike us as genuine problems. Contrariwise, an intellectus eliminates certain kinds of interests altogether by making them appear meaningless.

An example of the way in which a given definition of God governs an entire intellectus can be seen in the Augustinian conception of God as Eternity (necessary being). This definition focused the intellectual problematic of the early Middle Ages on the antithesis of the changeless to the changing. From this point of view, even goodness and truth were defined in terms of their power to endure in spite of the vicissitudes of time. The character of the world was defined as its corruptibility (i. e., its liability to be destroyed by time). Man's salvation from time was located in his power to contemplate unchanging realities. The image of God in man was located in memory, which is the seat of man's ability to transcend the temporal fragmentariness of existence and to see enduring and incorruptible forms. By this set of determinations the Augustinian conception of God as Eternity shaped the intellectus of an entire epoch. And there are other conceptions of God that focus the intellectus of other cultures on different problems. For example, the definition of God as "Being Itself" (or "Uncaused Cause") focuses an intellectus on problems of causality. The definition of God as "Person" focuses it on the distinction between consciousness and nature. The definition of God as "Sovereign Will" focuses it on the problems of power and authority. Because of the inseparability of a concept of God and a given intellectus, opposition to either one eventually generates an opposition to both.

PROPHETIC ATHEISM

5

Public atheism opposes an existing conception of God in the name of new concerns that cannot be given a right or satisfactory treatment within the intellectus which that conception establishes. This explains why periods of public atheism occur at moments of major cross-cultural contact. The atheism of the Greek *polis* broke out under the pressure of Persian cosmopolitanism. The atheism of the thirteenth century broke out when Christianity encountered Islamic science. In these cases, the dominant intellectus was able neither to handle nor even to recognize the new problems created by its contact with a new culture. Men who wished to deal with these new problems were therefore forced to reject the traditional conception of God and the intellectus that prevented their recognition. Insofar as it was concerned with new dimensions of truth and justice, the atheism of these transitional periods was prophetic—for it anticipated a later cultural epoch which would give these new concerns a proper place.

Concern with new problems is not the sole factor in public atheism. There are two other factors that intensify it, riding its coattails, so to say. In addition to opposition to a conception of God because of concern for new problems, there is an atheism that arises simply because of boredom with the traditional intellectus. This "atheism of boredom" arises whenever old problems no longer appear to be live issues. Such an atheism is different from the "atheism of concern" that springs out of a lively interest in a new set of problems. Hence, atheism of boredom arises not because of pressure upon a traditional intellectus from outside, but because a traditional intellectus dies from within.

A third factor in the literature of public atheism is sheer protest. This "atheism of protest" is neither able to overthrow a traditional intellectus by itself, nor truly desirous of doing so. For every protest derives its vitality from the affirmation it opposes. An example of atheism of protest is the symbiotic relation of teen-age atheists to their religious parents. The children's negation requires the parents' affirmation. Were that affirmation to die or to change, the negation would also perish. Such a symbiotic relation of negation to affirmation appears to govern the work of those "death of God" theologians who address themselves to no new problems but simply oppose the faith of the Church, their "parent." And because this atheism depends upon its symbiotic relation to this parent, it has nothing theologically important to contribute. It only seeks to shock.

Neither the atheism of boredom nor the atheism of protest has any prophetic significance, and in fact these two forms of atheism are always with us and do not occur just in periods of historical transition. Only the atheism of concern has prophetic significance and anticipates a new cultural epoch. This is because its honest concern for new problems and new truth drives theological understanding toward a new intellectus. Hence the attack on an old conception of God because it is inadequate to new problems also moves our minds toward a more adequate understanding of God.

By distinguishing the atheism of concern from the atheisms of protest and boredom, we can understand why many creative theologians have been accused of being atheists—for they sided with the concerns of the atheists of their day. Socrates was put to death on the charge of atheism. Thomas Aquinas' teachings were condemned as atheistic. Descartes, who accepted the skeptical principle of universal doubt as the starting point of his method, was even accused of atheism because he attempted to *prove* the existence of God. These men were charged with being atheists because they agreed with the concern behind the public atheism of their own day and rejected the received definition of God. But we see today that, in fact, the negations of these men were for the sake of their affirmations. They did not rest in their negations but sought out the affirmations that justified them. Through this search they came to formulate new definitions of God and new intellectus. Hence we speak of Platonism, or Thomism, or Cartesianism.

6

By understanding the historical significance of periods of public atheism we are helped to discover the prophetic significance of the "death of God" movement. Which "God" is dead and why? If we can specify the genuine concerns within modern atheism, we may be able to move towards the conception of God that will govern the next cultural epoch. For this new conception must be directed to these concerns and be able to legitimate them and help us deal with them.

Let us first take note of the fact that, because the secular theologians do not understand the historical significance of cultural atheism, they are unable to discover the new affirmation suggested by their negation. They are, indeed, even unaware that their negation suggests a new affirmation. For they believe that their negation of God can express itself in a secular culture, and they do not understand the inherent limitations of such secularism. Nor do they understand secularism's demonic character.

This lack of any unified understanding of the historical significance of atheism is evidenced by the disagreement among modern theologians about the "God" who is dead. According to Altizer, the "God" who is dead is the transcendent Totality whose very existence destroys the autonomy of the world. According to Cox, it is the God of rural religion and the God who is conceived metaphysically. On Pike's view, it is the Trinity. On Ogden's view, it is the God of St. Thomas, "Being Itself," to whom the world is related but who is not related to the world. Such a range of disagreement causes even the favorably disposed onlooker to wonder whether any genuine concern motivates these men, or whether theirs is only a particularly lively outburst of an "atheism of protest." But I believe that there is a genuine concern motivating the atheism of the present day, even though the secular theologians have been unable to agree on the character of the crisis.

I have already stated the principle to be employed in making our diagnosis. Any outbreak of public atheism intends to oppose the conception of God which governed the immediately preceding intellectus. This is why thirteenth-century atheism did not oppose "God in general," but attacked the conception of God affirmed by the immediately preceding intellectus, viz., God as Eternal. And sixteenth-century atheism did not oppose "God in general," but rather the conception of God as "Sovereign Will" which undergirded the authority structure of the immediately preceding period. Atheistic opposition to the "God" of an immediately preceding period arises, as we have seen, out of a concern for specific issues which cannot be handled within the intellectus of that period.

We can now apply this general theory in order to specify the prophetic element in modern atheism. Modern atheism intends to oppose the God who is conceived to be an individual person, possessing consciousness and will, who is separated from the world in the same way that individual persons are separated from each other, and who interacts with the world in the same way that individual persons interact with each other. Such a conception of God underlies the intellectus of the modern epoch (from 1600 A.D. to the present). It should be noted that opposition to God-as-a-person does not arise primarily because of theological difficulties in conceiving such a being—as if public atheism could be vanquished by showing that the best model of divine transcendence is the personal. Rather, it arises because such a God is the principle of an intellectus within which our new concerns cannot receive adequate formulation and honest understanding.

At the heart of modern atheism is an inability to believe in the existence of a Divine Individual Person who benevolently interacts with this world as one more member of the community. It is the denial of this kind of reality that creates a crisis for religion today and not the denial of the God of Thomas (Ogden) or the God of rural religion (Cox) or the God who is a sovereign Totality which destroys man's humanity (Altizer). For no one presently believes in such ancient deities anyway, and to deny their existence is not to be a modern atheist, but an antiquarian (just as the person who *disbelieves* in Roman deities is an antiquarian). The significance of modern atheism is not in its denial of conceptions of God that are appropriate to other cultural epochs, but in its denial of the God who is appropriate to our own cultural epoch: that is, the God who establishes the infinite value of individual personality, the God who undergirds democracy and capitalism, the God who makes empirical science possible. It is because modern atheism denies this God who underlies the modern intellectus that it is a prophetic principle of radical criticism.

THE DEATH OF THE MODERN PROBLEMATIC

7

We can understand the prophetic significance of modern atheism by focusing on the problem that underlies the growing opposition to the intellectus of our age. In so doing, we shall come to understand more clearly why modern atheism opposes the conception of God as a person.

Let us begin by characterizing the modern intellectus, since this provides the framework of the present crisis. The modern intellectus dates from the last major period of public atheism, i. e., from the radical skepticism of the sixteenth and early seventeenth centuries. The foundations of modern history were laid at this time, both in confirming the new concerns of this skepticism and in going beyond them to a new conception of God. Later developments in religious pietism and the Enlightenment did not negate, but strengthened and applied the constructive insights of the early seventeenth century.

When modern atheism of concern opposes the conception of God as a person, it does so because of an awareness of new truths, new forms of justice, and especially new problems which cannot be properly conceived or resolved within the intellectus of modern "Christian individualism." This intellectus is established on the principle that what is ultimately real is personal self-consciousness, the indubitable foundation, even the unrecognized presupposition, of all else. All else can be doubted, but the doubter cannot doubt himself. (*Cogito ergo sum.*) For everything else, to be is to be perceived—but not for the perceiver himself (*Esse est percipi*). The great creative theologians who established the intellectus of the modern world fought against skepticism. They overcame it by exposing the presupposition of all doubt, namely, the indubitable existence of individual self-consciousness.

The decision to regard individual self-consciousness as indubitable in principle creates the problematic of the modern intellectus: the opposition of nature and person, object and subject, is and ought to be. The boundary between these two realms follows the Cartesian distinction between what is dubitable and what is not. It is the distinction that determines the unique form of modern science, which regards nature, its object, as that which is dubitable—and this is the realm of fact, not values. Science, therefore, deals with what is, not what ought to be. But *this* distinction originates, as we have seen, in the Cartesian problematic.

The same Cartesian problematic determines the fundamental axioms of modern scientific method. Since it regards nature as the realm of the dubitable, modern science takes *contingent events* as its objects of study. The judgments of modern science are, for this reason, only *probable*. Moreover, they fall under this requirement for verification: scientific judgments are *falsifiable in principle*. It is with respect to these axioms that modern science differs from the science of preceding periods, and the axioms are determined by the problematic of our modern intellectus. Moreover, the scientific conception of all knowledge as constructive, or "controlling," also originates in the modern intellectus—since radical skepticism first eliminates all knowledge while the overcoming of skepticism requires that all knowledge be reconstructed. Thus we see that both the axioms of modern science and its theory of knowledge originate in the assertion that individual self-consciousness is the ultimately real basis of all else.

Not only do the axioms of modern science depend upon the modern intellectus, but so also do the axioms of modern morality. In our day both the certainty of moral judgments and the nonmoral character of "nature" are protected by establishing morality in some experience or activity of personal self-consciousness. Hence, modern morality is never *natural,* but is always *personal*—for nature is the realm of mere "facts" and values are now rooted in the person alone. In order to protect personal morality from subjectivism, the modern world asserts the universality of moral consciousness by grounding it immediately in God (Descartes, Kant). In this way modern culture identifies morality with religion in principle.

The unification of morality and religion in the modern epoch can also be evidenced by the typical modern proof of God's existence. Every epoch not only presupposes a determinate conception of God, but also establishes the reality of a being so conceived by means of a typical proof. The Augustinian intellectus created the ontological argument in order to prove the existence of an eternal good; the Thomistic intellectus created the cosmological argument in order to prove the reality of an uncaused cause; and the modern intellectus created the moral argument in order to prove the ultimate reality of universal moral consciousness. (The modern world also created a typical disproof of God: namely, the argument from evil and chance, which tends to show that universal moral consciousness is not the ultimate reality.)

The modern intellectus, like every intellectus, also generated unique institutions that express its problematic in consistent ways. In religion it created pietism and Protestant individualism, both of which glorify "the person of Jesus" or "the historical Jesus" as having the value of God. In politics it created democracy, which presupposes that society is artificially constructed from something more ultimate: individuals and their free consent and decisions. In economics it created capitalism, likewise an expression of the conviction that individuals are the primary productive units. In the intellectual order it created "the two cultures," the *Geisteswissenschaften* and the *Naturwissenschaften* —a consistent development of its person/nature problematic. It should be noted that this "two cultures" distinction underlies the contrast between *Geschichte* and *Historie,* the crux of Bultmannianism.

The person/nature problematic has allowed us to handle many kinds of problems, but it makes it impossible for us to handle others. Most importantly, it cannot integrate the new, third kind of knowledge which is beginning to dominate the intellectual life of our age. This new knowledge threatens to destroy the modern intellectus in the same way that Averroist science destroyed the Augustinian intellectus in the thirteenth century. And it is in the name of this new knowledge that a genuine atheism of concern has arisen to oppose the personal God of the modern intellectus.

8

Our outline of the basic characteristics of the modern intellectus allows us not only to locate the genuine problem animating the "death of God" movement, but also to eliminate false problems. A genuine problem is a problem which an intellectus is incapable of formulating or resolving in principle. It is crucial to distinguish between these problems (problems in principle) and false problems (which may be problems in practice). The "death of God" theologians have failed to distinguish between them, and, as a result, misunderstand the issue at stake in the cultural crisis of the present day. In order to distinguish the genuine problem of our cultural breakdown from the many practical problems that may cause religious difficulties for particular individuals, I shall quickly discuss three common arguments and show why they do not constitute the "problem in principle" that forces us to reject the idea of God as a person. Opposition to a personal God is not in principle required by any concern for (a) science, (b) the individual and his freedom, or (c) a new metaphysics.

a. No opposition to a personal God is required because of developments in natural science. We have seen that both the axioms and the conception of knowledge governing modern science presuppose the ultimacy of self-consciousness—which can doubt all else, but not itself. Hence, no protest against the existence or ultimacy of personal consciousness can be generated by arguments from natural science. "Person" and "nature" are correlative terms in the modern intellectus and are so defined that arguments appropriate to the one tend not even to bear upon—much less count against—the other. If anything is characteristic of our epoch, it is the discontinuity of these two realms rather than any supposed conflict between them.

The most striking fact about the relation between religion and science in the modern epoch has been the relative ease with which Christianity has integrated not only specific results of scientific investigation but even the sequence of scientific cosmologies that have been proposed over the past several centuries. This integration has occurred with such ease precisely because the theological principle for relating science and religion was fully clarified in the late Middle Ages. Since this is the case, we shall account for the fact that the most popular explanation of atheism is a supposed conflict between science and religion in the following ways: (1) There is always a tendency to interpret new conflicts as continuations of old ones. (2) There is a propensity to misunderstand the issues at stake in particular conflicts. Thus both the Galileo and the Scopes trials are assumed by many to be characteristic of the relation between religion and science in the modern epoch, whereas in both these cases the religious party was atypical. (3) There is an inclination to misunderstand the meaning of the historical process and to think it will culminate in a nonreligious scientific culture (e. g., Comte). (4) There is a tendency toward a sheer atheism of protest, within which one of the two major aspects of the modern intellectus is absolutized against the other. In this case, "scientific atheism" is symbiotically related to the individual self-consciousness that it opposes.

b. No opposition to a personal God is required by concern for individual self-consciousness, personal dignity, or the freedom of man. In fact, quite the contrary is true. The integrity of the individual person is protected by the affirmation that the principle of ultimate reality is a personal God. Such a correlation between the ultimate worth of individual persons and the personal character of deity is clarified by such philosophical personalists as Edgar S. Brightman. Where this correlation breaks down and God is conceived as, for instance, a God of race, we may have an Auschwitz. Therefore opposition to a personal God cannot arise out of concern for the integrity of the individual person.

The correlation of the idea of a personal God with the idea of finite persons can be illustrated in many ways. It is, for example, the basis of the claim that "persons" are of ultimate value. In modern philosophy, the discussion of the idea of a personal God turns quickly into a discussion of the reality and character of finite persons. So, for example, the defense of the reality of a self-conscious God turns quickly to an attack on, or defense of, the reality of finite self-consciousness. Or again, the attack on, or defense of, a personally *free* God is soon seen to hinge on the question of finite freedom. For example, Jean Paul Sartre, who contends that a free God presents a threat to my finite freedom, goes on to argue that even the coming of a finite free person into my presence constitutes a threat to me. *L'enfer,* he remarks, *c'est l'autre.*

Actually, to the extent that the contemporary *existentialist* protest against God depends on the recognition that all meaning and all certainty can be questioned (so that man must not accept the meanings society offers him, but must reconstruct all meaning for himself), it protests not against the ultimacy of a personal God, but against a metaphysical conception of God. But this form of atheism is not truly modern, since it repeats the skeptical criticism of the sixteenth century. Such skeptical atheism soon discovers exactly what Descartes himself proposed: that the value of doubt depends upon the ultimate dignity of personal self-consciousness. This is exactly what Camus concludes in the *Myth of Sisyphus.* So we see that existentialist atheism is not truly modern, since it takes as its enemy the metaphysical conception of God which was dominant in premodern Europe. Hence, the existentialist protest against God in the name of personal dignity does not create any difficulties in principle for the modern intellectus.

c. No opposition to a personal God is required because of any lack of interest in metaphysics (Cox) or because of any supposed inadequacy of classical metaphysics (Ogden). In the two preceding cases, we have seen that neither scientific nor individualistic atheism is in genuine conflict with the modern intellectus, although both may present practical difficulties for particular persons. Both Cox and Ogden suggest that the real reason for unbelief today is that metaphysics has lost its power. For example, Ogden explains modern atheism and secularism to be "the most extreme expression of a centuries-long reaction against the classical metaphysico-theological tradition of the Western world."[3] But such a proposal is incredible, for surely the significance of modern atheism lies in the fact that it rejects the God of the modern period of history rather than the God of

[3] Schubert Ogden, *The Reality of God* (New York, 1966), p. 16.

Thomas Aquinas (whom Ogden cites as the exponent of the classical tradition). The modern atheist is not in favor of Thomas' "Being
Itself," but he is not against it either. What he is against is the personal
God, the God of the modern epoch. Ogden fails to be convincing because his understanding of history is a mere figment of his polemic.
Moreover, his proposal is unable to do justice to the fact that many
modern secularists who oppose the conception of God as a person
feel themselves attracted to the Thomistic-Tillichian alternative, viz.,
the impersonal conception of God as Being Itself. I agree with Ogden
that this classical alternative to the idea of a personal God is inadequate
for the future, and I agree with his contention that metaphysics is
important. But I disagree with his claim that the reason for modern
atheism is that men are no longer satisfied with classical metaphysics.
Such a claim is unhistorical, and for this reason does not even
describe a practical difficulty behind modern atheism.

We have now excluded three interpretations of the problem in
principle behind modern atheism. Hereby we also reject those
theologies which focus their discussion in terms of concern for science
or for the integrity of the individual or for any kind of ontological
issue. That is, we believe that the problem of modern man is not what
Bultmann, Teilhard de Chardin, Tillich, Sartre, or Ogden have understood it to be.

HOT KNOWLEDGE AND COOL

9

Let us now come to that movement which presents a genuine threat
to the modern intellectus, a movement which forces its dissolution
and presages the emergence of a new cultural epoch. The name I
suggest for this movement is "sociotechnics." By sociotechnics is
meant that new knowledge whereby man exercises technical control
not only over nature but also over all the specific institutions that
make up society: i. e., economics, education, science, and politics.
Hence, sociotechnics presages the end of "economic man" as well as
of "scientific man" and "political man." It replaces these separated
institutional functions with the cybernetic integration of society within
a single rational system. Daniel Bell summarizes as follows the
character of this sociotechnical revolution, and its "defusing" of the
traditional institutions of the modern world:

It is part of a social transformation in which new attitudes about the world are being formed, attitudes as revolutionary, perhaps, as the idea of "experiment," which ushered in a Galilean as against an Aristotelian mode of thought, appeared to be in the seventeenth century. The heart of these attitudes lies in the idea of "Control," the growing awareness and knowledge of processes which allow us to regulate the wide variety of "systems" which are operative in the world: machine systems, economic systems, social systems, and eventually, perhaps, political systems.[4]

It is especially important to note that sociotechnics is replacing even politics as the dominant method of social control. Secular theology, which emphasizes the "political" character of Christianity, is therefore out of touch with the revolution of our time. As such, the political proposals of the secular theologians—far from helping us to overcome the problem of our time—only intensify our misunderstanding of it. Such a criticism also applies to classical Marxist "theology," which emphasizes economics as socially decisive.

The term *technē* designates an art or technique that can be exercised in order to control an environment. The classical conception of technique presupposes that the technician will be an artist whose creations either follow or idealize nature. The new conception of technique, however, is different. It presupposes that nature will follow art; hence technique is a transforming activity governed not by man's experience of nature but by his imaginative insight. For this reason, the sociotechnics of our time anticipates the creation of a wholly artificial environment. An entire society will organize in order to reshape itself and its world in accordance with an imaginative vision of the good life.

The reason for calling this new movement sociotechnics rather than technology is to oppose the popular theory that technology is intrinsically related to natural science. We so frequently encounter the phrase "science and technology" that we have come to think of technology as the fruit of scientific endeavor. But this is not the case. Technology uses science in the same way Newton used Arabic numerals and computation procedures. Technology is not created by science; it is the invention, rather, of those social thinkers who sought not to advance science but to create a new form of social organization. This desire to create a new social organization is what differentiates contemporary sociotechnology from the *technē* of the ancient Greeks.

[4] Leon Bagrit, *The Age of Automation,* preface by D. Bell (New York, 1965), pp. xi-xii.

Sociotechnical knowledge is neither an art nor a science. Rather, it is a *tertium quid,* whose methods and criteria are wholly new. Consider, for example, how the psychologist, or sociologist, or historian, or manager investigates his material by taking up a position within it. In this participational attitude, the "positional" subject-object stance —characteristic of the disciplines of the modern intellectus—is overthrown. The investigator actually influences his subject matter by his questions (as in the effect of pollsters on elections), yet his questions are also affected by the answers he receives. On the basis of his participation, there is a continuing cycle of inquiry and feedback, which culminates not in "facts" but in "images."[5] These images are the basis for a rational system of control. Because the investigator does not stand outside the system, but is a part of it, the modern subject/object distinction does not arise. The sociotechnical disciplines have *no particular point of view.* They are neutral, for the sociotechnician who controls the system is also being controlled by it (the "feedback" phenomenon). This does not mean that the sociotechnical methods are arts rather than sciences. They are, rather, a wholly new discipline, one which utilizes participation in order to know. Marshall McLuhan has referred to the "cool" character of modern media.[6] We can extend his metaphor and say, also, that the sociotechnical methods are the new "cool" disciplines. They can be clearly distinguished from the "hot" natural sciences of the modern epoch which were based on the subject/object split.

The intention behind sociotechnics becomes clearer in a cybernetic age, when rational techniques are applied not only to the production of goods from nature but also to the organization of the very society which produces and consumes these goods. Hereby the economic, political, and educational systems themselves become the objects of sociotechniques that seek to minimize irrational stress and to maximize rational unity. Pollsters, psychological testing, and economic indicators all become the information-gatherers of the sociotechnicians; the media of public communications play an ever more crucial role in society as they are devoted to the manufacture of opinion which contributes to the rational stability of the new system. It is this sociotechnical goal of rational control of the social system

[5] Cf. Kenneth Boulding, *The Image* (Ann Arbor, 1961), esp. ch. 11.
[6] Cf. Marshall McLuhan, *Understanding Media: The Extensions of Man* (New York, 1965), esp. ch. 2. "Hot media are, therefore, low in participation, and cool media are high in participation or completion by the audience" (p. 23).

that contradicts the modern intellectus. For sociotechnics regards the free decisions of individuals as mere *quanta* to be ordered within the system of mass society, "the compass of rationality itself." What sociotechnics seeks

> . . . is the unlocking of a social alchemist's dream, the dream of "ordering" the mass society, a society where daily, millions of persons make billions of decisions on what goods to buy, the number of children to have, the kind of house to build, what trip to make, for whom to vote, what job to take. Any single choice may be as unpredictable as the quantum atom responding erratically to the measuring instrument, yet the aggregate patterns are to be charted as neatly as the geometer triangulates height and horizon.[7]

The developing cybernetic society is destroying all the "holy ultimates" of the modern world by what Marcel calls "the spiritual and intellectual crimes attributable to what one might call a sort of *pantechnicism. . . .*" He suggests that "from the point of view of the individual in such a society, there is no conceivable way out at all: private life, as such, does not exist any more."[8] The new sociotechnical movement displaces the ultimacy of individual self-consciousness and free choice. In subordinating these values to sociotechnics, it also rejects the conception of a transcendent personal God who undergirds them.

The opponents of the sociotechnical movement of our time are not intellectual dinosaurs, but are, in fact, persons who have achieved a general reputation for being astute social commentators. Gabriel Marcel, Karl Jaspers, Erich Fromm, David Riesman, William Whyte, and many others defend the modern conception of the ultimacy of the individual and his inner-directedness. The nature of their protest can be seen in a list of chapter titles from a recent book collecting their essays: "The Fight Against Totalitarianism," "Individualism in Suburbia," "Man Is Not a Thing," "The Invasion of Privacy: Technology and the Claims of Community," "The Person Alone," "The College Student in an Age of Organization," "Bureaucratic Structure and Personality," "The Individual's Demand on Society," and so on.[9] These critics all oppose the fusion of man and machine in sociotechnic mass society. In the view of the sociotechnicians, however, this in-

[7] Bagrit, *op. cit.,* p. xiii.
[8] Gabriel Marcel, *Men Against Humanity* (London, 1952), pp. 52, 8.
[9] *The Dilemma of Organizational Society,* H. Ruitenbeek, ed. (New York, 1963).

C

dividualistic protest against technique is merely a "pseudo-religious insistence that some kinds of activity are proper to sentient creatures alone."[10] Thus the pantechnicism which is emerging in our time appears to be destroying the individual person and overthrowing the "holy ultimates" of the modern period of history.

In their sustained opposition to the cybernetic revolution of our time, many liberal critics reveal a surprisingly unhistorical attitude. They do not even acknowledge the inevitability of the transformation that is taking place. This transformation is inevitable because the knowledge of the sociotechnics is more powerful than the old arts and sciences of the modern world, and is capable of helping us to deal with critical problems of our age—problems the modern world has generated but has not been able to solve. The cultural transformation that is taking place is therefore as inevitable as the transformation of Augustinian culture under the impact of Islamic science or the transformation of late medieval culture under the impact of individualism and the empirical sciences. A more profound and penetrating rationality has been discovered, and the "modern intellectus" is being overthrown by it.

10

The rise of the sociotechnic intellectus has created special problems for *Protestant Christianity,* for Protestantism is an integral part of dying modern culture. It is Protestantism that gave religious sanction to individualism and to those institutions that presuppose individualism: capitalism, democracy, and romantic marriage. It is Protestantism that seized upon the invention of printing to create a religion of the book and a service of worship centered not on the ritual enactment of a myth, but on the exposition of the meaning of a written text. It is Protestantism that stripped nature of its moral telos, rooting morality in an immediate relation between the individual and God. Protestantism—its theology, ethics, institutions, and spirituality —is an integral part of modern culture, shaping and being shaped by it. The passing of the modern age creates, therefore, a special crisis for this form of Christianity.

In this situation, Protestantism has two options. (1) It may follow the example of the early Christian Church (in the moment when its expectations for an imminent return of Jesus failed) and can radically revise its theology, its worship, and its institutional life. (2) Or it may

[10] Stafford Beer, *Cybernetics and Management* (New York, 1964), p. 25.

follow the example of sixteenth-century Catholicism, which, faced with the demise of her familiar medieval milieu, refused to enter fully into the life of the new modern culture and entered upon its defensive "Tridentine stage." Will Protestantism be bold enough to give up its privileged position vis-à-vis modern culture and strive with others toward an uncertain future? Or will it enter into its own Tridentine stage by attempting to maintain the values and form of modern culture —even as that culture disintegrates? I am inclined to think that the latter will be its fate; institutions seldom give up privileged positions and vested interests, even in dying cultures. But there is a chance that Protestantism might learn enough from history to change her direction. For history, as a sociotechnic discipline, helps a man gain some understanding of the reasons why he is the way he is, and, thereby, gives him the opportunity to become other.

Through historical study of the social and psychological factors that shaped it, Protestantism might begin to recognize the degree to which its understanding of the Word of God is merely an articulation of the assumptions and values of modern culture. Protestantism's lack of historical consciousness, its docetic leap from the first century into the sixteenth (when the gospel was "rediscovered"), inclines it to a simplistic identification of the forms of modern culture with the gospel itself. This is not to say that Protestants have not pioneered the historical study of religion. They have, but they have always studied religion at some comfortable remove from their own origins. The Protestant knows that the Pentateuch was not written by Moses, that the Trinity is a hellenization of Christianity, and that Anselm's *cur deus-homo* presupposes feudal conceptions of honor. But he does not know that his so-called "Biblical view of history" actually is a consequence of the typographic "visualization" of time as space, and that his high valuation of personal self-consciousness is simply the projection of seventeenth-century philosophy into Scripture. Protestantism has been historically critical with regard to the religion of others, but historically naïve with regard to its own religious claims.

Although a sense of the discrepancy between its religious faith and the emerging forms of sociotechnic life has provoked a vocal self-criticism among Protestants, this self-criticism has not been therapeutic. For it has thus far been carried on in intellectual modes that misrepresent the problem. The death of God theologians discuss the crisis as if it were only religious—rather than a crisis affecting the entire culture with which Protestantism is identified. Such criticism cannot help them to cope with the problem, for it misrepresents it. To cope with the crisis, it must be understood historically, sociologically, and psychologically, i.e., as a crisis in the culture with which Protestantism is identified and for which she has provided special religious sanctions. Robert Bellah, commenting on *Honest to God*, makes this point with special clarity when he says

The problem for Robinson and for those he represents is that they are trapped in their own theological language. They know something is wrong, but they have no means to get outside and see what it is. They talk about taking the world seriously but do not do so. They don't, at least not seriously enough, ask what the world has found out about man, society, symbolism and religion. They don't ask how this might help the present urgent need for reinterpretation of symbols.

Here is the sort of answer I would give if I were asked: We have not begun to understand the full implications of religious language and symbolism. Social science has not begun to fathom the deep insights into human motives and human action that the religious tradition contains. But we do know that religious symbols are the way man has, from the beginning of his existence as a cultural being, related himself to the conditions of his existence. Through religious symbols man has symbolized to himself his own identity and the order of existence in terms of which his identity makes sense.[11]

Bellah locates the religious problem of the present in our failure to recognize the social function of religious symbols and in the failure to bring the social sciences to bear upon this problem. His proposal is that we regard the present crisis in religion as part of a complex social crisis. He criticizes the secular theologians for discussing the problem of faith as if it were separable from a general crisis of culture. It is because they separate the crisis in faith from the crisis of culture that they tend to think the next epoch in history will be simply "the modern world" minus traditional religious faith; i. e., they anticipate the rise of a wholly secular society. But such an expectation is as naïve as the secular theologian's interpretation of atheism itself. For it fails to see that the crisis of the present day involves the disintegration of the structures of the entire modern world under the pressure of the sociotechnic movement.

[11] Robert Bellah, *"Honest to God:* 'It Doesn't Go Far Enough,' " *Christianity and Crisis* 23 (1963), p. 200.

THEOLOGY FOR A SOCIOTECHNIC AGE

11

It is impossible within the framework of this chapter to develop a sociotechnical theology. My purpose has been simply to locate the genuine problem at the heart of modern atheism and to suggest the direction in which theological development must go. However, we can anticipate several characteristics of a new theology for the coming age.

1. Theology must develop a conception of God which can undergird the primary realities of the cybernetic world, viz., systems. And ethics must reorient its work in terms of these systems and focus on the problem of control. Cybernetics is concerned with the control of probability systems whose terms are the manifold decisions of free individuals. Just as the personal God of the modern intellectus undergirded the ultimate value of individuals, so the God of a sociotechnic intellectus must be reconceived as the unity of the manifold systems of the world. Such a God will not only be the encompassing whole, and the principle of individuality, but most importantly He will be the unity of an encompassing system of relations. Such a conception of God has already been developed by earlier American theologians whose vision of God was essentially social. They saw God as the unity of community, the principle of loyalty, the metaphysical tendency towards a holy and righteous world, the One who establishes the existence of society. It is not an exaggeration, I believe, to claim Edwards, Emerson, Royce, and H. R. Niebuhr as advocates of such a theocratic hope.

To move toward this conception of God as the unity of the encompassing system of social relations will not require a development in Christian doctrine, but only an application of doctrine that already exists. Christianity already speaks of God as the unity of a social system when it calls the Holy Spirit the unity and reality of the Church. The Holy Spirit is God as a social system within which individuals have their life and make their decisions in harmony with other individuals.[12] Such a conception of God as the unity of a social system is radically different from the modern conception of God as a person, explicated by a theological emphasis on the historical Jesus. But this shift to a social conception of God is required for any theology

[12] A fuller discussion of this point is given in ch. 5, sec. 6 f.

that will be adequate to the new sociotechnic age. It should be noted that the secular theologians of our time have not developed their conception of God in a way adequate to the new social problems; rather, they persist in an individualistic emphasis on the historical Jesus.

2. The theological emphasis, not upon divine totality nor upon divine individuality, but upon divine relationality leads to a second characteristic of sociotechnical theology. The total cybernetic system must be fortified by an eschatological symbolism which can provide it with general goals and assist men to make the continual transitions an increasingly complex system requires. A cybernetic system determines a rate and form of change, but it does not determine the ultimate end of change. Rather it is guided by some encompassing social vision of the good society. This vision cannot be conceptually precise—for then it would be static rather than dynamic. But it must be symbolically precise if it is to give real direction to the social process.

The American philosopher Charles Peirce has helped us to understand the guiding power of a myth or symbol which must be conceptually "vague" if it is to guide rational development.[13] Such a "vague" symbol is open to continual conceptual specification; hence it is capable of providing direction to a total cybernetic society. It is conceptually imprecise, but symbolically precise. Such symbolism must be religious, i. e., it must portray a transcendent kingdom of God. The very transcendent character of religious eschatology is the condition of its adequacy for guiding a cybernetic society; for transhistorical symbolism always retains the "vagueness" and conceptual openness that prevent man from expecting any absolute fulfillment in time. Only transcendent religious symbolism can undergird an infinite development of society at a controlled pace. Only "otherworldly" religious symbolism can preserve the system from falling into an intrahistorical stasis. The very conceptual vagueness of these symbols is what makes them meaningful and socially useful. The secular theologians, by their repudiation of eschatological transcendence and by their rationalization of religious symbols, again show their total misunderstanding of our historical situation in rejecting the

[13] Charles Peirce, *Collected Papers*, C. Hartshorne and P. Weiss, eds. (Cambridge, Mass., 1960), V, par. 505, p. 355 f. "A sign is objectively *vague*, in so far as, leaving its interpretation more or less indeterminate, it reserves for some other possible sign or experience the function of completing the determination."

very aspects of religion which are essential to the new sociotechnic age.

3. A sociotechnic theology must develop new ethical principles which will enable men to live in harmony with the new impersonal mechanisms of mass society. This ethic will affirm the values of a technical social organization of life in the same way that earlier Protestantism affirmed the values of radical individualism and capitalism. In proposing this new style of life, sociotechnical theology must reject that anarchic individualism which opposes all social structures in principle. The very independence and competitiveness which were virtues in the modern world are vices in a sociotechnic world where other-directedness, teamwork, and conformity to *the systems of society are necessary conditions for the optimum organization of human life. Critics of the sociotechnical revolution continue to despise these virtues of the new epoch in the name of individual freedom, nonconformity, and uniqueness. In their writings the terms "team man," "conformity," and "organization" are used as epithets. In this way, they render men less capable of dealing with the new problems of the world, for they encourage the maintenance of those individualistic virtues which now impede right action. They also thereby increase the feeling of guilt in men who, having been taught the older moral theory, are now attempting to adapt to the technological world.

In their opposition to sociotechnical culture, the representatives of both the new left and the old right are united. But they should know that the virtues they extol are historically relative. These virtues replaced those rejected by the Protestantism of the sixteenth and seventeenth centuries: humility, self-sacrifice, celibacy, obedience, and silence. These other medieval virtues were appropriate to another kind of society. They were formulated with the ideal of monastic life in mind. In monastic communities, where persons live in continuing close relation to each other such that the community and not the individual is the primary social unit, such virtues maintain the harmony of life. The Protestant opposition to them was justified by the emergence of a new cultural epoch. Today, our rejection of the moral theory we inherited is based on the same recognition that we are entering a new era, when the fundamental social unit will be man-and-machine: the cybernetic system.

4. Theology must create new liturgical forms and new myths whereby the unity of sociotechnical life can be presented and experi-

entially "felt" by all men. The vastness and complexity of the culture of the coming epoch will be such that few individuals will ever be able to understand the processes that shape their lives. Unless, therefore, the meaning of the system can be portrayed and participated in through some liturgical representation, individuals will undergo the kind of personal disintegration that destroyed the victim in Kafka's *Trial*.

The function of liturgy is to present a concrete embodiment of the whole in which we live. By participating in the liturgy, men come to feel themselves a part of this whole and discover through it the meaning of life. Hence, liturgy—far from being irrelevant in a cybernetic society—will be a necessary instrument for the maintenance of meaningful life. Historians appreciate how the new liturgies developed by Protestantism since the Reformation have supported and clarified the meaning of life for modern men. There is the same need for new forms of liturgy which will support and clarify the meaning of sociotechnic life, to give men a "feel" for its meaning.

The emerging sociotechnical civilization has already begun to create new myths and liturgies. For example, professional sports increasingly play a liturgical function in contemporary life, since they bind complex communities together in a single ritual act and a common group loyalty. At the same time, these sports provide an object lesson in the increasingly specialized character of modern "team" life. Sociotechnic culture has also given rise to such mythic heroes of comic books and television as Batman and Superman, whose legends have become an integral part of the contemporary ritual.[14]

Myth and ritual not only bind men together in complex communities of loyalty, but they also shape the psychic attitudes of persons to the "time" of society. In a sociotechnic world, new myths will be needed to shape the psychic life of persons to the new flow of time.[15] For example, traditional Hinduism offers a myth of the flow of the life process. It divides life into four periods: the time of the student (a period of chastity), the time of the householder (a period of marriage and child-bearing), the time of the forest dweller (a period of withdrawal from private family life in order to be a community "elder"), and the time of *sannyasi* (a period of withdrawal to prepare oneself

[14] Mircea Eliade, *Myth and Reality*, W. Trask, trans. (New York, 1963), pp. 184-87.

[15] For example, see Edward Hall, *The Silent Language* (Greenwich, Conn., 1966), ch. 1.

for death). The seven sacraments of Roman Catholicism also imply a linear flow of life: from baptism to confirmation to marriage to sickness and eventual death. But the rate of change in a sociotechnic society will be so rapid that these older myths will no longer be adequate. When, for example, each person has to be completely reeducated three times in his life, it will be nonsense to think that marriage should *follow* education. The chronological time of older civilizations is being destroyed by the very rapidity of social change. Hence, the old myth of the life process must be replaced.

It should be noted that the earlier Protestant attack on the seven sacraments of Roman Catholicism in favor of the two sacraments of baptism and Communion already has involved such a reunderstanding of the flow of the psychic life process. One social result of this Protestant reinterpretation is modern man's repugnance toward the process of aging, and his refusal to cease work and accept the "naturalness" of death. The same kind of mythic reexpression of the ideal flow of the life process is also required by the coming technological world.

12

In developing the categories and methods for thinking about the cultural revolution of our time, Christian theology should turn first to the American social and religious tradition. For it is America that has created and continuously promulgated social technology. Max Lerner has perceptively expressed the American vision of life in the following words:

The Big Technology has been for Americans what the Cross was for the Emperor Constantine: *in hoc signo vincas* [sic]. It set the pace for an impressively swift and thorough conquest of a new environment and of world leadership. The American has been a machine-intoxicated man. The love affair (it has been nothing less) between the Americans and their Big Technology has been fateful, for it has joined the impersonal power of the machine to the dynamism of the American character. As by some tropism of the spirit, the Americans have followed out the logic of technology all the way. The world has seen civilizations based on very different principles: on beauty and an equipoise of living, on otherworldliness and reality of the supernatural, on close personal allegiance, on military prowess, on ascetic control of the self. But in each case the principle was embodied mainly in the life and outlook of an elite group. Never before has the motive principle of a civilization spread so pervasively through all strata of its population, so completely changing the lives of its ordinary people.[16]

America is very frequently described as the land of individualism and personal freedom. I myself am inclined to think that this is a misrepresentation of the actual state of affairs. There is no doubt that individual freedom is a major ingredient in our cultural life— just as individualism is a major ingredient in the life of all nations affected by the Enlightenment. Moreover, this individualism and personal freedom is more obvious in America than in the life of other western nations, for America is the sole major nation whose political foundations were established in modern times. However, after all these things have been acknowledged, it is still true that what is uniquely characteristic of America is not what she shares with modern Europe, but her faith in social technology. The vision of a wholly artificial environment, man and society together restructured by the power of the machine, is the American dream. And Christian eschatology has undergirded and sustained this dream from the earliest beginnings of our life as a nation.

That sociotechnics is characteristic of American life can also be shown by the fact that this discipline is primarily an American creation. Every cultural epoch generates a unique kind of knowledge which expresses its spirit. The Greeks created the liberal arts; the Middle Ages created philosophical theology; modern Europe created the natural sciences. America has created a new kind of social knowledge: the disciplines of sociology, humanics, and management; the techniques of psychological testing, cybernetics, and mass communications. Thus theology must draw its understanding of the coming epoch from an analysis of this new kind of knowledge that has flourished in America.

Not only has America created sociotechnics, but it has also encouraged the growth of this new knowledge by a consistent tradition of theological and philosophical theorizing. William Ames, "the father of American theology," is the earliest representative of a brilliant tradition of theological thinking which regarded the world as intrinsically malleable by social techniques (a view quite different from the modern concept of a formless reality in process). Bushnell, Dewey, and Reinhold Niebuhr have expanded this tradition and have

[16] Max Lerner, "Big Technology and Neutral Technicians," *The Dilemma of Organizational Society*, p. 77 f.

provided the basis for social experimentation. In pragmatism, American philosophy has created essentially a social epistemology. American religion is especially characterized by its constant efforts to create new institutions for effecting moral renewal and social reform: Finney's revivalism, Rauschenbusch's social gospel, King's civil disobedience. At these and other points, the American theological and philosophical tradition is a rich lode for those who wish to shape the coming age.

13

My proposal that Christianity affirm and shape a sociotechnical intellectus is not based on any preference for this intellectus, but on a recognition of its inevitability. Theology need not fear to move in this direction, for it is not confined to any particular cultural expression, but is rooted in a divine revelation. Just as, from the perspective of this revelation, theology has previously shaped a Christian Platonism, a Christian Aristotelianism, and a Christian individualism, so it can and will shape a Christian sociotechnicism. Theology can do this because it is rooted in a revelation which contains the fullness of truth and because it knows that every created intellectus is a partial expression of that fullness.

Not only can Christian theology undertake this task, but it must undertake it. The sociotechnical intellectus requires the same religious foundation that the individualistic intellectus required in order to be redeemed from its own peculiar demonic tendency. Every intellectus requires a religious foundation if it is to sustain itself as the principle of a cultural epoch. It is not an accident that atheism is merely a transitional phenomenon, for an atheistic culture is impossible in principle. The attempt to establish an atheistic culture fails because an absolute denial of God finally negates its own negation.

For these reasons, the task of theology is not only to affirm the new concerns implied by the prophetic atheism of a transitional moment in history, but also to resist their secularization. In providing a religious integration for a new intellectus, theology also works to redeem that intellectus from the destructive power of secularism. In the following essay I shall take up this problem, giving special attention to the peculiar form of secular idolatry that threatens to distort or destroy the sociotechnical intellectus of the coming age.

II

Five Kinds of Faith

NONBELIEF VS. FALSE BELIEF

The purpose of this chapter is to discriminate various kinds of belief and unbelief in order to explain the sense in which relativism is "unbelief" and the need for opposing this attitude with a new form of faith. First, then, we note that the term "unbelief" is ordinarily used in two quite different senses. "Unbelief" may indicate a nonbelief, i. e., a mere lack of belief. For example, when a mother will not believe a report that her son is dead, we say, "She heard the news with unbelief." On the other hand, "unbelief" may indicate not a lack of belief, but a false belief. In this case, the word is used like "untruth" in the sentence, "He spoke an untruth, i. e., a falsehood." For example, when materialism is called a "philosophy of unbelief," this is understood to mean that a false belief is being affirmed rather than that belief per se is lacking. Of course, the proponent of a "philosophy of unbelief" may reply that his so-called false belief is really no *belief* at all, for it is based not on faith, but on knowledge. We acknowledge the legitimacy of this objection and shall deal with the problem it raises in a later section of this chapter. For the moment it is sufficient, however, to note that such an objection presupposes a prescriptive notion of "belief," whereas we are here concerned with the variety of meanings associated with the ordinary usage of the term "unbelief." We shall call the mere lack of belief "unbelief[1]" and a false belief "unbelief[2]."

The two kinds of unbelief involve assertions that have logically different characteristics. Unbelief[1] is asserted by means of a negation,

30

i. e., "I do not believe T." Unbelief[2] is asserted by means of an affirmation, i. e., "I believe F." We call both types of assertions "unbelief" because both deny what ought to be affirmed as true. But, the former does so immediately, i. e., by simply negating it; the latter does so by way of consequence, i. e., by affirming what ought not to be affirmed, it implicitly denies what ought to be affirmed. So, for example, an affirmation of the Trinity can simply be rejected on the grounds that there is no evidence to commend such an assertion as true, or an affirmation of the Trinity can be denied on the grounds that such an assertion is excluded by other affirmations we have made. There are, in fact, theological categories for distinguishing these two types of unbelief with respect to God: the former is "atheism," the latter is "idolatry."

Formally considered, atheism is a negation, while idolatry is an affirmation. Although a negation presupposes an affirmation, it does not assert an affirmation. Rather, it denies an affirmation. For this reason, the meaning of a negation is contained wholly within the affirmation that it denies. In discussing atheism, certain contemporary theologians have shifted the level of their analysis away from the existential significance of an atheist's assertion to the question of its linguistic meaning. Rather than acknowledging that by means of an existential negation an atheist categorically rejects a theistic affirmation, these theologians argue that since the *meaning* of every negation is derived from the affirmation it opposes, every atheist implicitly affirms that which he explicitly denies in his very act of denying it. Atheism, they conclude, is self-contradictory, for since we cannot assert that God does not exist without using the affirmation "God does . . . exist," all atheists must affirm God's existence in the very act of denying it. This argument is utterly fallacious—although it has almost become common opinion in certain circles. But it should be noted that theologians are not solely responsible for this situation. Rather, the recent philosophical movement that muddied a crucial distinction by asserting that the verifiability of propositions is also the criterion of their meaningfulness contributed to this confusion.

The argument that a man implicitly affirms the existence of God when he denies that God exists is wrong because it surreptitiously confuses the meaningfulness of the proposition "God does not exist" with a judgment about a matter of fact. In this way the atheist is said

to believe that God actually exists because his denial of God's existence presupposes the statement "God exists." But to assume that a
proposition is meaningful in the course of denying that what it asserts
to be the case is not the case involves no self-contradiction. If it did,
then it would not only be self-contradictory to deny the affirmation
that God exists, but also to deny any other existential affirmation,
e. g., "It is snowing" or "There is a tree." Hence, by a banal confusion of language and reality, every existential negation becomes self-
contradictory. It may, of course, be the case that some kind of
ontological argument can be developed to show that the denial of
God does involve a self-contradiction. But this would only be the
case if "God" were not like "snow" but could be shown to be a
unique concept.

A second common fallacy in the discussion of atheism confuses the
logical status of the atheist's denial of God with the psychological
or historical process from which this denial arises. For example, it is
sometimes argued that the atheist's denial of all transcendence is a
"Christian attitude" since, historically, this atheism was able to arise
only after the biblical teaching that God absolutely transcends the
world had become widespread. Or again, it has been argued that
because western civilization developed partly from Christianity, whoever affirms western civilization also affirms Christianity since western
civilization would not have developed without it. Or again, since
profound psychological unbelief occasionally arises from revolt
against the belief of another (e. g., against "the Faith of our Fathers"),
the former implicitly affirms the latter since it would not have occurred
without it. All these arguments confuse the logical status of the
atheist's denial of God with psychological and historical accounts of
the process by which a person comes to make an assertion. They
confuse these two, for unless it can be shown that the validity of an
existential assertion is necessarily dependent upon the psychological
process by which one comes to understand and make such an assertion,
then it cannot be contended that all western atheists are logically
committed to affirming Christianity in some way or another. If such,
in fact, were the case, then every person who had a pirate in his
genealogy would also be committed to affirming piracy. But this is
sheer nonsense. The confusions encouraged by certain contemporary
theologies on these points need desperately to be dispelled—for there
is no greater insult to a man than to tell him that whether he affirms
God or denies God, he thereby confesses that God exists.

By distinguishing the logical and the psychological accounts of the status of atheism from one another, I do not mean to depreciate the significance of the latter. Rather, the distinction is made for the sake of discussing atheism as a legitimate psychological problem in its own right. Precisely because every negation does logically presuppose the affirmation it opposes, it is legitimate to assume that every atheist acknowledges there is a basis for discussing what he denies to be the case. He is open, not closed, to theological debate. And when we begin to discuss his assertion with him, then it is important to understand not only its formal status, but also what he understands it to mean, why he has come to this conclusion, and what kinds of psychological and sociological "practical objections" need to be overcome before its purely formal truth or falsity can be a matter of direct attention. For, in every concrete case of atheism, what is at stake is not simply the formal truth or falsity of an assertion, but the concomitant psychological and sociological factors which make the formal assertion believable, attractive, or repulsive. It is, I suggest, because the psychological and logical factors are so intertwined in every argument for or against God's existence that such arguments "never convince anyone."

Each of the philosophical systems that emphasizes psychology rather than logic, i.e., that is primarily interested in an analysis of how the mind actually operates in the process of knowing rather than with an analysis of the formal status of assertions, offers its own account of the place of atheism within the psychology of mental life. So, for example, Platonism, with its dualistic correlation of being and non-being, will show the indissoluble symbiotic dependence of atheistic negations on theistic affirmations within psychic life (e. g., this is Tillich's method). Hegelianism, with its description of reason as a movement whereby contradictions in knowledge are transcended in new unifying syntheses, will note the dialectical denial of limited concepts of God for the sake of ever more encompassing notions. And existentialism, with its uncovering the nothingness at the heart of life, will interpret the atheists' negation absolutistically, i.e., as the sheer "no" of total despair or infinite freedom.

I suggest that each of these philosophical psychologies has a basis in human experience. Each can be correlated with one of the three types of atheism mentioned in the first chapter. In Platonic psychology, the "no" is related to the "yes" dualistically and remains symbiotically dependent upon it. This relation of negation to affirmation is found in the "atheism of protest" that is a natural stage in the intellectual development of youth—whose denial of God depends upon the continued affirmation of God by their fathers. This dependence is evidenced by the fact that the strength of the negation is commensurate with the strength and vitality of the affirmation it opposes. Such "atheism of protest" seems to be rooted in a psychological need to establish an independent identity over against a dominant culture. It thereby precedes and makes possible the appropriation of a mature affirmation of God as one's own. It is with this understanding of the relation of negation and affirmation in mind that the Socratic dialogical pedagogy is formulated, and theologians should use this method for dealing with all "atheisms of protest."

In Hegelian psychology, the "no" is related to the "yes" not dialogically, but dialectically. The "no" seeks to negate the "yes" by becoming a new affirmation that goes beyond it. This dialectical denial of God is found in the "atheism of concern" that rejects a received concept of God because it contradicts (or seems to contradict) some new truth. In this case, the denial of an older affirmation is for the sake of some new affirmation. Such "atheism of concern" seems to animate many mature scientists and reformers, i.e., those who are committed to intellectual and moral truth. Because the negation of this atheism is for the sake of new truth, it should be met not by dialogue, but by genuine theological reconstruction.

In existential psychology, the "no" is absolutely separated from the "yes" and made into a new principle of total despair or utter freedom. To this psychology are correlated the nihilistic and/or utopian atheism of our and every time. In such atheism, the denial of God expresses spiritual uprootedness, sense of the imminence of death, and disgust with the meaning of ordinary life. Whether it is dying with a bang or with a whimper, this denial of God can be met by neither dialogue nor theological reconstruction, but only by pastoral concern and love. For in this case there is ever a certain irrationality within the negation itself which shows that we are dealing not with a "dead God," but with a broken soul.

Our discussion of the three psychological types of atheism presupposes that the negation of God with which we are dealing is unbelief[1], i. e., it is a mere lack of belief whose logical expression is through a negation that is open and indeterminate with respect to what actually exists. In this respect, unbelief[1] differs from unbelief[2], which is closed and determinate with respect to what actually exists. It is important for theology to distinguish between these two forms of unbelief. Atheism is a *tertium quid* between theism and idolatry. It is a state of unbelief that does not affirm any particular existence, since no existential affirmation is entailed by any existential negation. In this sense, then, it differs radically from that unbelief which is sin, namely idolatry. We shall now turn to a discussion of this second kind of unbelief.

FIVE SECULARISMS

We have seen that idolatry is that form of unbelief which expresses itself through an affirmation that is false and which excludes, by implication, various other true affirmations. For example, someone who says that all reality is composed of atoms is implicitly committed to the affirmation that no spiritual realities exist. Idolatry is unbelief of this kind, and the Christian faith regards idolatry as sin—not because idolatry is false (for atheism is also false), but because idolatry is destructive of man's true humanity. As we shall see, however, the concept of idolatry and its relation to Christian faith is much more complex than that of atheism, and it is to this problem that we now turn.

The modern name for idolatry is "secularism." Secularism is an attitude towards reality by which men live (think, act, feel) as if the world existed through itself alone. When men attempt to live as if the world existed through itself and as if it were not open in all realms of life to the energies of God, then they curve the cosmos and themselves in upon themselves. The expression of this "incurvedness" (which is Luther's word for describing the sinful state of man) is the absolutization of a particular limited understanding of things. Man begins to measure life by his own definition of "meaning" and "relevance." And since, in fact, the world is open to God and is not exhausted within a single intellectus, the result of the secularist program is to generate hostilities against, or to exclude from consideration, all aspects of life that are not amenable to this simple principle. So the Neo-Platonists despised the natural just as the Averroists denied the supernatural. In each case, the limited first principle led to the rejection of some part of life, for the principle itself was not sufficiently rich to unite all things.

D

Paul Tillich has noted the demonic tendency implicit in all secular attempts "to capsule the inexhaustibility of being within itself."[1] I am going even further in suggesting that this destructive tendency, especially pronounced in the secularism of today, expresses itself in overt hostility to some aspect of reality. Strictly speaking therefore, secularism finds itself unable to encompass all being within itself, and, because it is unable to achieve its ambition, seeks the reason for its failure elsewhere. Whatever reason it fixes upon becomes its scapegoat: the communists' capitalists, the capitalists' communists, the city folks' country folk, the country folks' city folk, et ad exterminationem. Only if we regard secularism as sin can we have an adequate interpretation of the evil in the world.

There are as many types of idolatrous unbelief as there are cultural intellectus. Since every secular attempt to encompass all reality in a given intellectus not only must fail, but also become demonic, Christianity attempts to open and to redeem every intellectus by correlating with it an appropriate kind of faith. For this reason, there are as many kinds of faith as there are kinds of intellectus. And we do not understand the meaning of faith unless we understand the particular redemptive function it is attempting to achieve within the intellectus of its day.

Every cultural epoch is characterized by a dominant intellectus, which undergirds not only the thought of an age but also its institutions. Since intellectus themselves are relatively unique, there will also be social institutions in some cultures for which there are no parallels in other cultures. For example, in ancient Near Eastern culture, the function of the naqam (vindicator) was institutionalized—an institution which has no parallel in American culture. This fact—that different intellectus give rise to unique institutions—is of considerable importance for my thesis, for I shall later argue that the contemporary relativist intellectus is characterized by the unique institution of ideological conflict.

I shall limit my discussion of faith and intellectus to five major correlations of these terms as they occur within the Christian era. In these five correlations, the following intellectus are at stake: mystical rationalism, scientific naturalism, skeptical criticism, gnosticism, and relativism. Each of these major forms of intellectus has dominated

[1] Cited from James Luther Adams, Paul Tillich's Philosophy of Culture, Science, and Religion (New York, 1965), p. 51.

a given cultural period, and each found its classic opponent in some Christian theologian who opened it to divine transcendence by correlating it with an appropriate notion of faith. In each of the five the form of faith is different, since the form of faith is determined by the tendency of the particular intellectus it opposes. And every form of faith involves a different way of understanding divine transcendence.

1. *Fides quaerens intellectum.* This most widely known way of correlating faith and intellectus was formulated by the Augustinian tradition. While the best-known representative of this view is Anselm, the fundamental problematic stems from Augustine. In the formula *fides quaerens intellectum,* the intellectus is mystical rationalism. Such an intellectus conceives meaning to be that which is grasped by the purified reason as it ascends, by means of dialectic, to mystical union with God through the *nous.*

According to Augustine, the defect in this view of intellectus is that it fails to come to terms with the role of the will in the work of understanding. The ascent toward a mystical knowledge of God generates a kind of *superbia,* or pride, which intrinsically contradicts the moral purity necessary for mystical union. By generating *superbia,* mystical reason destroys itself. This contradiction can be overcome only if reason seeks the *nous* in humility, and this requires that humility and the *nous* be united—as they are in the incarnation of Jesus Christ. When one thinks with the humility of Christ, one is then able to "rise" to union with the *nous* without contradiction. By this criticism, Augustine redeems the mystical-rationalist intellectus from the defect of pride. Hence, in the phrase *fides quaerens intellectum,* the term *fides* means that *humility* which is the only appropriate attitude for seeking mystical union with Truth. Such humility is the transcending reality which the mystical-rational intellectus could not encompass and to which it had to be opened.

2. *Fides perficiens intellectum.* The scientific-naturalistic intellectus is manifested in its classic form in thirteenth-century Averroism. This scientific intellectus understands the meaning of things to consist in the objective knowledge of nature as a closed system (in contrast to the mystical-rationalist desire for knowledge of, and union with, the supernatural *nous*). The classic opponent of scientific naturalism is Thomas Aquinas, who correlates a new notion of faith with it. The Averroist intellectus did not purport to lay hold of God or to lead men to eternal beatitude. Rather, it denied both that nature has a

Creator and that man has a destiny beyond nature. The defect of this intellectus is not its *superbia,* but its denial that the desire of the human soul for eternal beatitude can ever be fulfilled, or perfected. This Averroist denial resembles the contemporary Freudian assertion that man's desire for a life to come—however deeply it may be rooted in the human heart—is based on an illusion. In the Averroist rejection of a more-than-natural, we see the characteristic secular rejection of some aspect of human life, i.e., the inevitable manifestation of secular man's inhumanity to man.

In opening and transcending the scientific-naturalistic definition of intellectus, Thomas redefines faith. Because this scientific intellectus has only the world, and not God, as its object, the faith correlated with it does not need to be a "seeking faith," for scientific understanding, which is not moving towards God as its object, needs no supernatural help. (For example, an immoral chemist can be just as good a chemist as a moral one.) Rather, faith needs to complete, or perfect, scientific knowledge by adding to it the belief in or assent to those supernatural realities for which the soul of man longs and which scientific understanding can neither know nor seek. By asserting that *fides perficiens intellectum,* Thomas changes the conception of faith from a humility which seeks and assists the understanding, to a belief which affirms those supernatural realities that are the beatitude of man. This belief preserves the scientific intellectus from its demonic tendency to treat men as if they were only natural functions and not souls with eternal destinies. By his redefinition of faith as belief in supernatural reality, Thomas opens scientific understanding to divine transcendence and thereby redeems it from demonic misuse.

3. *Fides formans intellectum.* Late medieval scientific intellectus collapsed before the skeptical criticism of the Renaissance, the *Que sais-je* of Montaigne. We have not, I believe, given sufficient attention to skepticism as a distinctive form of secular intellectus. But this skeptical intellectus generates the most radical secularization of life. The intellectus of skeptical criticism (including the skepticism of contemporary existentialists like Camus) consists not in knowing, but in not-knowing. In its opposition to human knowledge of God, skepticism is willing to deny even human knowledge of man and of the world. In this situation, there is no need for *fides quaerens,* for there is no understanding to be sought, and there is no need for

fides perficiens, for there is no understanding to perfect. Skepticism is hostile to everything except its own confidence that the meaning of life is its meaninglessness. This is the basis of radical nihilism.

The classical theological opponents of skepticism are Pascal and Jonathan Edwards. They oppose this skeptical destruction of intellectus by redefining faith and its work. To redeem man from skepticism, we must invoke faith as a power which gives every intellectus its foundation and its power. According to Pascal and Edwards, faith is the work of the heart, which gives reason its own first principles. *Le coeur a ses raisons que la raison ne connaît point.* The heart gives reason not only the formal principles of identity and noncontradiction but also the desire to know. In this way, skeptical reason is transcended by invoking its divine ground. Skeptical reason is transcended in the direction of depth, for faith creates a possibility for understanding by manifesting the ground of meaning in the face of skeptical reason's own shallow despair. In our own day, of course, Paul Tillich has elaborated the idea of faith as a power to show anxious intellectus its divine ground. And this has been Tillich's device because his primary intellectual opponents have been the existentialist skeptics of our time. In this *fides formans intellectum* we see a third way to speak of divine transcendence.

4. *Fides crucificiens intellectum.* The discussion of gnosticism as a secular intellectus has been left to this point because I have wished to call attention to an error made by some contemparary theologians. These theologians make a simple identification of the Gnostic intelllectus which Paul opposes (in First Corinthians) with every form of intellectus. For example, Ernst Käsemann makes this mistake when he asserts that all philosophy and science involve some attempt by man to transcend his finitude in order to save himself or justify himself before God. Käsemann assumes that the Pauline discussion of faith and wisdom describes the *perennial* relation of these two terms.[2] But it should be clear by now that this is a nonhistorical reading of the problem, which fails to come to terms with the distinctive intellectus of our own time.

The Gnostic intellectus which Paul opposed was a secret saving wisdom. Later Gnosticism was not only a secret wisdom but a wisdom whose first principle absolutely contradicts both the Christian Creator

[2] This view was presented and defended by him in lectures and discussions at Harvard in 1966.

God and His creation. Hence, Paul described the relation of faith and intellectus as an absolute opposition: *fides crucificiens intellectum*. The opening of life to God in the face of a secular gnosis (which claims to know God (but knows a false god) can be achieved only when this gnosis is overthrown. Such an absolute opposition of faith to intellectus becomes necessary whenever the Church confronts not skepticism, or scientism, or rationalism, but gnosticism. This is what occurred in our own time when the German Church at Barmen confessed Christ alone and set Him in absolute opposition to Hitler's neognosticism. Only by crucifying a gnostic intellectus can life become open to God. The kind of faith to be correlated with gnostic wisdom, therefore, is not humility, is not belief, is not the depths of feeling, but is the foolishness of the gospel, the paradoxical claim that through death comes life.

FIDES RECONCILIANS INTELLECTUM

5. Faith opens relativistic intellectus to divine transcendence by affirming an invisible power of reconciliation working in all things. The formula *fides reconcilians intellectum* indicates the point at which Christian theology should press the apologetic enterprise today.

While every cultural epoch has some dominant intellectus, this is not to say that there may not be subordinate, and even competitive, themes in a culture. So, for example, we have already seen that Tillich's theology is oriented towards the existential skepticism of our day, just as Barth's theology in the thirties was opposed to the neognosticism of National Socialism. But even if we admit there are such subordinate themes, it still remains the case that we are seeing the rise of still another dominant intellectus, one that affirms the socially relative character of all judgments. This insight has been pursued relentlessly in the characteristic disciplines of the present day: history, sociology, and psychology. For example, a thesis common to other western epochs—namely, that man has direct access to God through conscience, or has an objective access to reality through knowledge—has been systematically denied by the relativistic intellectus, which works to extirpate every nonsocial and nonideological dimension of human understanding. In this situation, all language is affirmed to be political rhetoric, all concepts are reduced to images, and all explanations are historico-genetic.

Now relativism, like all the previous intellectus we have considered, not only attempts to set itself up as the sole arbiter of reality (eliminating divine transcendence) but also has its own distinctive demonic tendency. In order to specify this tendency, let us employ a simple typology for which no other claim is made than its usefulness in allowing us to compare the five terms I have presented. The distinctions made by this typology deal with (1) access to knowledge: public or privileged, and (2) object of knowledge: natural or supernatural.[3] With these terms, we can compare the five sets as follows:

	supernatural object	natural object
privileged access	gnosticism	relativism
public access	mystical rationalism	scientific naturalism
no access	skeptical criticism	

From this diagram, we see that relativism is like gnosticism in that it affirms knowledge to be acquired only in a privileged way; but relativism is like scientific naturalism in that it claims the object of knowledge to be natural. The peculiar demonic tendency of relativism arises from the combination of these two factors. With respect to the fact that it affirms access to knowledge to be privileged and not public, relativism posits the same irrevocable and irreconcilable separation of the *cognoscenti* from outsiders that is found in gnosticism. But whereas the gnostic object of knowledge is supernatural, the relativistic object of knowledge is natural. Whereas gnosticism asserts an opposition between the natural and supernatural orders of reality, relativism asserts an opposition within a single natural order

[3] The term "supernatural" does not here mean "above man's nature" in the strict sense, for both mystical rationalism and gnosticism ascribe a spiritual capacity to man whereby he can know realities that transcend ordinary sense experience. The term "supernatural" is coined from the scientific naturalistic perspective, which affirms that direct knowledge of spiritual realities is "above man's nature" in the strict sense. Hence, all five options in the diagram affirm that which is necessary to a secular denial of the necessity of faith, viz., they all affirm an isomorphism between human capacities for knowledge and all the reality that exists to be known.

between those who truly understand the meaning of life and those who do not understand the meaning of life. In this way, modern relativism generates a unique institution: ritual ideological conflict. This conflict is ritualized because it is undertaken both because of and in order to confirm ideological commitments. It is not, in fact, conflict over particular problems; hence it is unresolvable in principle.

Eric Voegelin has noted the rise of this ideological conflict in the modern world and explains it as the result of resurgent gnosticism. My analysis both confirms his judgment and goes beyond it. For I agree with Voegelin regarding the kind of "gnostic" knowing that characterizes the modern world; but by introducing a second set of considerations, I show how this privileged knowing generates radical intramundane conflict—something not characteristic of religious gnosticism. Modern relativism brings the dualism which is characteristic of religious gnosticism down into the natural order of time and space. In this situation there is inevitably conflict, for there is no basis for peaceful coexistence among parties which are ideologically opposed.

Faced with the inevitability of ideological conflict, the relativists have replied that conflict is not only a necessary but also a valuable part of life. They say that it creates values rather than destroying them. Conflict not only encourages pluralism and diversity; it even creates or strengthens such values as justice, brotherhood, and equality. This position is held by many persons today, but in order to see it in its sharpest form let us consider the assertion of Adolf von Harnack, the Church historian, that the most extreme form of human conflict—war itself—sustains such values as freedom, equality, and brotherhood. Addressing an audience during a period of war, Harnack said:

What is the situation today with respect to these three values? First, freedom. My friends, have we not had a feeling of freedom burning within us ever since the day that the war began? Has not this feeling become stronger in the midst of oppression and need? How can we account for this? It has happened because when a situation concerns freedom—and especially when it concerns our freedom and existence—then the will for freedom arises and shines most brightly. What is freedom, then?. . . . Freedom is for a man gladly and wholeheartedly to do what he should do. It is for him to want to do what he must do. . . .

Second, equality. Death is a great equalizer. But it is sad if a society knows no other equalizer than death. But now another equalizer has arisen: war. For even war is a great equalizer. . . . The spirit of comradeship in which officers care above all for their men and men care above all for their leader is the true heartwarming spirit of equality. This spirit is always found in an army, but war brings it out with double sharpness. . . .

And the third good, brotherhood and unity. How differently each man regards his countryman today! Someone marches off to war, and it may soon be the case that he has died for you; so you feel a sense of reverence as you watch him march away. . . . Great sacrifice creates deep brotherhood. Once again we can understand something of those great ideas that in duller times lay meaningless and powerless about us, or were even mocked—ideas like sacrifice, satisfaction, and substitution.[4]

Harnack's contention that war sustains rather than destroys human values has been echoed in the fascism and communism of our time. But the relativistic intellectus so pervades the world today that conflict is glorified not only by the extreme right and the extreme left; it has been increasingly structured into the whole fabric of modern culture. (a) Ideological conflict has been institutionalized among modern nations by doctrines of inevitable war, total struggle, and unconditional surrender. Such theories are proposed not only by totalitarian dictators but also by many adherents to the democratic world view. (b) Ideological conflict is institutionalized within nations as political factionalism, the right of revolution, and the purely disruptive protest. (c) It is institutionalized in the economic order as strikes. We may recall that it was only a little over thirty years ago that strikes were made a legal method of resolving disputes between management and labor. (d) In the racial order, ideological conflict is institutionalized as segregation. (e) In the academic world, it is institutionalized by scientific specialization and departmental competition.

In short, the relativistic intellectus has justified and institutionalized not only social differentiation and cultural pluralism but also ideological conflict. Because this conflict is institutionalized, it is undertaken for ritualistic reasons, i.e., to confirm one group's ideological enmity toward another.

Faced with this demonic tendency, the Church must oppose relativism with a faith which will open it to a transcending redemptive reality. In the four previous cases of *fides/intellectus,* we have seen

[4] Adolf von Harnack, *Aus der Friedens- und Kriegsarbeit* (Giessen, 1916), pp. 319-23.

that faith is defined by being coordinated with the defect in a given intellectus. Now, if we seek a conception of faith which is appropriately correlated with relativism, we shall define faith as the power of reconciliation which works to unite the many relative perspectives and to thwart ideological conflict. In this context, faith is the commitment of man to oppose the separation of man from man. It is a commitment to struggle against attacks on the common good, against racialism and segregation, and against the fragmentation of man's intellectual and spiritual life. Such a conception of faith characterizes the thought of certain creative contemporary theologians. The most important Catholic theologian in this new movement is Bernard Lonergan, who ascribes to faith the specific function of transcending the ideologies and separations that impede man's disposition toward unity. The most important Protestant proponent of a theology of reconciliation is Martin Luther King, who has developed this theological principle into a new method for effecting social change.

In our time, therefore, faith affirms reconciliation in opposition to the relativistic intellectus which denies its possibility. In intellectual discussion, faith expects agreement and not only dialogue. In war, faith expects and works for peace. In economic struggle, it calls for the common good. In the working together of Churches, it anticipates ecumenical reunion. In all these acts, faith affirms something the intellectus of relativism cannot see, i.e., the power of divine unity working in all things to reconcile the ideological conflict generated by relativism itself. Quite concretely, too, faith as the affirmation of such a power of reconciliation also affirms that all those institutions and movements of our time which are working to overcome ideological conflict are special instruments of redemptive power. One thinks immediately of the United Nations, the Peace Corps, the worker priests, federal mediators, and ecumenism. These are the institutions where God is working in the world today, but only the *fides reconcilians* will have the eyes to see. Other forms of faith not only will fail to discern God's working at these points, but may, because of their irrelevance, surreptitiously encourage the demonic tendencies of our time.

To conclude, therefore, let me illustrate how the analytical scheme presented in this chapter assists us in specifying the notion of an "irrelevant faith," a faith which not only is unrelated to the intellectus of its day but which, because it is unrelated, may even support the demonic propensities of that intellectus. In the table below, let S^{1-5} be the five forms of secularism we have discussed and let F^{1-5} be the five forms of faith. Then the correlations we have considered can be arranged as follows:

(gnosticism)	S^1————F^1	(*crucificiens*)
(rationalism)	S^2————F^2	(*quaerens*)
(naturalism)	S^3————F^3	(*perficiens*)
(skepticism)	S^4————F^4	(*formans*)
(relativism)	S^5————F^5	(*reconcilians*)

Now suppose that we encounter a Christian whose working intellectus is S^5, but whose faith takes the form of F^1. In this case, of course, such a person may reject F^5, i.e., reject the form of faith which opposes the destructive tendencies of the relativistic intellectus. Might it be said that, in spite of affirming F^1, such persons are really "unbelievers" because they do not affirm the form of faith that is appropriate to the intellectus of their day? It should be noted that such a question is not purely fanciful, for there is a group of contemporary New Testament scholars who hold the Pauline antignostic conception of faith and yet adopt the methods and conclusions of historicism in their work. In dealing with certain aspects of the world, therefore, their faith makes no difference. On these points, they operate just as the relativists do.

If this illustration is too academic, then consider the more poignant case of the pious Christian who affirms F^3, the supernatural *fides perficiens,* while all about him racism, war, and other ideological conflicts work their destruction. The conception of faith formed in the earlier confrontation between Christianity and scientific naturalism now becomes an impediment to the faith needed for overcoming the secular idolatry of another age. And surely both Protestants and Catholics have equal share of persons who are practicing racists (S^5) while also believing *supernatural truths* (F^3). From this we see it is possible for the same man to be both an unbeliever and a believer at the same time; i.e., he may affirm S^5 while also affirming F^1 or F^3.

The same point should also be pressed against all secular criticisms of faith. It is, for example, not uncommon to find a given secularist criticizing the form of faith appropriate to *another* intellectus. Such a method not only guarantees a win—for what is being rejected has no intrinsic point of connection with the secularist's intellectus, but it also serves to distract attention from the limitations and destructive tendencies implicit in that intellectus itself. So, for example, the historicist has no difficulty showing that supernatural *fides perficiens* is irrelevant, and by his discussion of this false issue, he avoids the pressing question of a *fides reconcilians*.

BEYOND RELATIVISM

The analysis of relativism and ideological conflict brings us now to the question of the relation between these and the sociotechnical intellectus discussed in the first chapter. We can specify this relation as follows.

1. We have seen that each of the five intellectus discussed in this chapter—gnosticism, mystical rationalism, scientific naturalism, skeptical criticism, and relativism—has attempted to absolutize itself in a secularism that excludes faith in a transcendent reality.

2. We have seen that the idolatrous attempt to absolutize a secular intellectus generates a particular form of man's inhumanity to man. That is, the creature's idolatrous attempt to capsule all meaning in a finite matrix generates hostility against those realms of life that cannot be encompassed within the terms of that matrix.

3. We have seen that Christian faith has not opposed, but has accepted, the various cultural intellectus. But it has accepted them only by qualifying them. That is, Christian faith has correlated an appropriate conception of faith with each of these intellectus in order to redeem them from their anti-human tendencies.

4. The following formula may therefore be stated: a secular intellectus plus a specific form of faith yields a Christian, or religious, intellectus. This can be illustrated as follows:

  a. mystical rationalism + humility → Christian Platonism
  b. scientific naturalism + belief → Christian Aristotelianism
  c. skeptical criticism + sense of the heart → Christian individualism
  d. gnostic wisdom + the foolishness of the cross → Christian fideism
  e. relativism + universal reconciliation → Christian sociotechnicism

The sociotechnical intellectus requires, as we have seen, the possibility of reconciling, or mediating, all conflicts among men within a single cybernetic system. This presupposes that the consciousness and activity of every individual is social or socializable, so that every individual act will fall within the system of control. A cybernetic society avoids the use of coercive political power since coercion presupposes that some individual actions fall outside the system of rational control. For example, a cybernetic society attempts to handle school desegregation by controlling the flow of government school subsidies, industrial contracts, and location of federal employees rather than by sending in troops. The assumption is that control over the complex pattern of interests will lead finally to a rational adjustment to national norms. Although a cybernetic society will still utilize coercive power when the system of control breaks down, its long-range goal is to reduce such practical failures to a minimum, on the assumption that every individual action is ultimately socializable.

The relativistic insight regarding the social character of all human consciousness and activity underlies the sociotechnic program. But the problem, as we have seen, is that relativism cannot move from its assertion that man has a social nature to the conception of a society as a noncoercive, universal system of control. This is because relativism asserts that the particular social factors conditioning consciousness and action so vary from group to group as to make a universal social system impossible. In fact, we have already seen that relativism actually generates the opposite of sociotechnical noncoercive control, namely, ritual ideological conflict. In this we see how a secular intellectus turns against, and eventually destroys, its own first principle: relativism begins by discovering the social nature of man and ends by destroying the very possibility of society.

In order to maintain the relativistic insight regarding the social nature of man, some way must be found to universalize it and thereby establish the basis for reconciling every conflict of interest. In this way, sociotechnical community can come into being. But this universal reconciliation can be brought into the relativistic intellectus only by something that goes beyond it, namely, by faith in reconciliation, or faith that reality is, in fact, a unity. It is this faith that underlies sociotechnical community.

The faith that makes sociotechnical universalism possible generates a new form of *speculative* reflection, which parallels the practical knowledge of such sociotechnical disciplines as sociology, history, and management. This speculative reflection is metacriticism: that is to say, thought which takes other thought as its object. It attempts to transcend the socially relative ways of thinking of particular social groups in order to understand the basis of their various claims and thereby reconcile their different interests. For example, when Martin Luther King attempts to effect reconciliation between whites and Negroes, his action must be based on a metacritical understanding of how both whites and Negroes think. This understanding does not claim to possess *another* social perspective which is "raceless"; rather, it seeks to transcend particular forms of social thinking in order to bring all particular forms of social thinking into a single system. Such thinking makes use of what Marshall McLuhan calls "the principle of suspended judgment."[5] And McLuhan is correct in noting that the emergence of this kind of thinking marks the beginning of a new kind of human consciousness.

An important example of the way the metacritical principle of suspended judgment works to universalize relativism is the sociology of knowledge. This new discipline begins with the recognition that all primary knowledge is ideological in character because it expresses the vested interests of a particular social group and cannot transcend this limited perspective. Sociology of knowledge attempts to overcome ideology by developing the idea of universal social knowledge, i.e., developing the kind of knowledge presupposed by a sociotechnical system. Let us consider an example: Karl Mannheim, perhaps the major figure in the development of this new metacritical discipline, argues that the coming age requires a "transition from the theory of ideology to the sociology of knowledge."[6] This transition is necessary, he notes, because the relativistic intellectus cannot reconcile disagreements, but always interprets them as the result of *falsches Bewusstsein* —the false consciousness of a "totally distorted mind which falsifies everything which comes within range."[7] To ascribe a *falsches Bewusstsein* to one's opponent is to assert the impossibility of settling a disagreement or reconciling a conflict with him because all his thought expresses class interests that are opposed to a universal society. Hence, he must be segregated, or destroyed. This is the basis of all ideological conflict. In this situation what are we to do? Mann-

---

[5] *The Gutenberg Galaxy* (Toronto, 1962), pp. 71, 278.
[6] Karl Mannheim, *Ideology and Utopia*, L. Wirth and E. Shils, trans. (New York, 1936), p. 75.
[7] *Ibid.*, p. 70.

heim replies that there are two possibilities. We can stop with relativism, or we can go beyond it to a nonevaluational, metacritical conception of knowledge. Such a metacritical knowledge will allow us to understand the many relative points of view and to reconcile them within a single nonevaluative sociology of knowledge. However, Mannheim acknowledges that this reconciling knowledge cannot be attained merely by empirical sociological analysis. It is on a higher level, one which involves an "unavoidable, implicit ontology." This is the level to which the fifth form of faith belongs: the *fides reconcilians* that affirms the possibility of unifying a multiplicity of intellectual perspectives. Such a faith, or such an "unavoidable, implicit ontology," defines "the horizon within which lies our world of reality and [it] cannot be disposed of by simply labelling it ideology."[8] Here, says Mannheim, we finally see a glimmer of a "solution" to the problem of relativism. He thus acknowledges that relativism creates a problem which can only be overcome by the introduction of a new understanding of transcendence.

In the fourth chapter in this volume, I shall attempt to delineate the kind of philosophy that McLuhan and Mannheim are calling for. It utilizes "the principle of suspended judgment" (metacritical consciousness) to transcend the many competing ontologies and reconcile them in a new principle of unity. Before taking up this problem, however, we shall, in the intervening chapter, consider another aspect of sociotechnic culture more closely. We shall discuss myths and how they unify and reconcile a specific kind of human experience. Such myths are as important a part of religion as is faith, and the peculiar character of myth in the sociotechnic intellectus is its high degree of differentiation vis-à-vis the other modes of understanding. This consideration of myths in terms of both their unifying function and their differentiation from other types of understanding will lead us naturally into the kinds of questions dealt with later in this book.

8 *Ibid.,* p. 88.

III

The Myth Is the Message

DEMYTHOLOGIZING OR DIFFERENTIATING?

1

The theory that man's intellectual life has evolved from religious myth through rational metaphysics to empirical science underlies not only Cox's proposals in *The Secular City,* but also Rudolf Bultmann's insistence that Christianity must translate the original mythical expression of the Gospel into a language consistent with the scientific world view. The theory that man is evolving toward a totally nonmythical way of understanding claims an important evidence in its favor, namely, the rapid growth of the empirical descriptive sciences. Scientific thinking strives to understand the world by reducing the rich composite whole of ordinary experience to its simplest terms. These terms can then be described within an impersonal reference system which can, in principle, be understood even by a machine. Such a reference system utilizes neither myth nor metaphor; it requires neither affection nor valuation in the scientist.

Though I agree with this understanding of the growth and character of scientific knowledge, I cannot concur that the development of this knowledge shows that man is evolving towards a nonmythical, non-poetic way of understanding his world. The demythologizing theory of history is wrong because it identifies empirical science with all understanding. Actually, the modern world is characterized not only by the growth of empirical science, but also by the rapid development

of two other kinds of understanding: (1) the purely theoretical knowledge of logical and mathematical relations, and (2) the purely imaginative knowledge embodied by aesthetic symbols, myths, and actions.
The modern world is not only the world of the verification principle;
it is also the world of *l'art pour l'art* and Gödel's theorem. Moreover,
the social effects of all three kinds of knowledge have been felt in our
time. For example, ours is the first age when myth has been understood and consciously employed in order to manipulate an entire
people into a course of action which they rationally abhorred.

   To the demythologizers' hypothesis that the evolution of human
understanding moves from mythical religion to empirical science,
I would propose an alternative explanation: that man's intellectual
development has moved from an undifferentiated to a differentiated
kind of thinking. It is not the case that primitive thinking is wholly
mythical. Rather, in primitive thinking, empirical descriptions, rational
hypotheses, and myths all interpenetrate one another in an undifferentiated way.[1] None of these aspects of understanding is eliminated
during the historical development of human understanding. They all
persist. But man first distinguishes them, then orders them, and—in
the modern period—finally separates them into independent realms.
This is why the purely empirical interests of modern science are
paralled by the purely aesthetic concerns of modern nonrepresenta-
tional art. This is why Ayer's verification principle is paralleled by
Baudelaire's principle of imagination. This process of intellectual
differentiation has made both scientific knowledge and mythical
knowledge increasingly powerful.

                                   2

Historians and phenomenologists of art, literature, and religion call
attention to the function of myth in modern society, and their observations are corroborated by psychological and sociological research.
Gerhard Lenski's *The Religious Factor* shows that religious commitments and interpretations of life play a major role in determining the
political, economic, and educational decisions of urban people. Again,

   [1] "The imagery of myth is therefore by no means allegory. It is nothing less
than a carefully chosen cloak for abstract thought. The imagery is inseparable
from the thought. It represents the form in which the experience has become
conscious." H. and H. A. Frankfort, *et al., The Intellectual Adventure of Ancient Man* (Chicago, 1946), p. 7.

E

the sociologist Robert Angell describes the "moral web" of society, which is (and must continue to be) undergirded by myths and rituals: "Common values need hands and feet, so to speak, and ritual, myths, and heroic figures serve in that capacity."[2] Moreover, historical sociologists show that myth functioned in past societies in the same way that it functions today. Hannah Arendt's study of Roman civilization and Henri Frankfort's studies of Near Eastern civilization present impressive corroborations of this fact.

The proponents of a demythologizing theory of intellectual evolution reply to these sociological and historical findings as follows: The empirical studies of Lenski, Angell, Frankfort, and others do describe the *present* state of society—for ancient myth and ritual possess tremendous residual power which enables them to persist in spite of the new forces that work against them. But how, these critics ask, can we conclude from these empirical descriptions of the present-day function of myth that mythical thinking will continue to play the same vital role in the society of tomorrow? The world is historical; therefore it is always changing. So how can descriptions of yesterday and today be a basis for a prediction about the future?[3]

The reply to these questions is as follows: (1) The prediction that mythical thinking will continue to play the same important social function in the future as it has in the past is on a better footing than the alternative prediction of the demythologizers because it rightly claims a certain probability in its favor. Sociological studies of many different modern societies, together with historical studies of many different past civilizations, show that myth persists and plays the same social function even in cultures that are radically different. This constitutes a legitimate basis for predicting that a future society will also be integrated by myths and religion. (2) The demythologizers reply to this argument, however, that the future will be different from the past because man's way of understanding his world is changing. The development of modern science, they assert, is an evidence that man's thinking is becoming less mythological. But we have already seen that the demythologizing theory of man's intellectual development takes into account only one kind of modern knowledge, omitting such things as mathematics and art from consideration. The differ-

[2] Robert Angell, *Free Society and Moral Crisis* (Ann Arbor, 1965), p. 28.
[3] For example, Cox offers this argument. See *The Secular City Debate*, D. Callahan, ed. (New York, 1966), p. 116.

entiation theory, on the other hand, not only accounts for the rise of modern science, but also for the rise of other ways of thinking. Hence, the demythologizing theory of history has less claim to truth than the differentiation theory because it does not account for as many data.

The proponents of a demythologizing theory of history now press another argument, namely, that if sociology contradicts the program of demythologizing, then sociology is not scientific but ideological! Harvey Cox articulates this criticism. He asserts that those sociologists whose studies lead them to conclude that urban society is "made up of symmetrically stable components of religious and profane" hold to "a kind of homeostatic theory, very common in contemporary sociology, but certainly not byond criticism. The critics of homeostatic theory say that although it makes sense of systems and stability in a society, it has trouble dealing with authentic change and newness. Some of its critics would even maintain that homeostatic social theory betrays a conservative ideological bias. It can be used to rationalize stability and *status quo,* to oppose change."[4]

Though he may not agree with all these criticisms, Cox seems at least to argue that an open, changing society cannot be integrated by myths, since myths integrate societies by closing them from change. Myths create "static, tribal societies." But such an argument is incorrect. It does not follow from the fact that static, tribal societies are integrated by myths that changing open societies cannot also be integrated by myths. In fact, some social theorists argue that a cybernetic society requires more (not fewer) myths and images in order to maintain the process of change. For example, Kenneth Boulding concludes his discussion of the effect of cybernetics on human life by suggesting that the future vehicle of both social integration and social change will be "images."[5] And Marshall McLuhan suggests the similarity between "myths" and "images" by relating them to the older concept of "icons." "The pictorial consumer age is dead," he writes. "The iconic age is upon us."[6]

In the new electric age of information, the backward countries enjoy some specific advantages over the highly literate and industrialized cultures.

[4] *Ibid.*
[5] Kenneth Boulding, *The Image* (Ann Arbor, 1961), esp. ch. 6-8.
[6] Marshall McLuhan, *Understanding Media: The Extensions of Man* (New York, 1965), p. 167.

For backward countries have the habit and understanding of oral propaganda and persuasion that was eroded in industrial societies long ago. The Russians had only to adapt their traditions of Eastern icon and image-building to the new electric media in order to be aggressively effective in the modern world of information. The idea of the Image, that Madison Avenue has had to learn the hard way, was the only idea available to Russian propaganda. The Russians have not shown imgination or resourcefulness in their propaganda. They have merely done that which their religious and cultural traditions taught them: namely, to build images.[7]

In this way, both Boulding and McLuhan argue that the new cybernetic society, which will presuppose continual planned change, must be integrated by myths and images precisely because it cannot be organized for change in any other way.

3

Our discussion of the social function of myth raises certain theoretical questions. How should we understand myths themselves? What reality do they speak about? How are they meaningful? Such theoretical questions are at the center of the theological movement which seeks to demythologize the Christian faith. The major figure behind this movement is Rudolf Bultmann. However, rather than considering Bultmann directly, we shall contrast our position with that of the most radical proponent of demythologizing, the American theologian Schubert Ogden.

Ogden, like Bultmann, contends that myth speaks about reality "by making use of terms and categories that in principle misrepresent that reality."[8] Ogden argues therefore that "to claim that a given mythical assertion is true, although not literally so, is to commit oneself to state the meaning of the assertion at some point in other, nonmythical terms."[9] Ogden finds these other nonmythical terms in the language of a relational ontology. He asserts that we must restate the meaning of a myth in an ontological language which properly expresses its meaning so that we can understand what the myth intends to signify and judge whether it is true.

Ogden distinguishes between religious faith and philosophical ontology, making the truth-claims of the former dependent upon the truth

[7] Ibid., p. 343.
[8] Schubert Ogden, The Reality of God (New York, 1966), p. 117.
[9] Ibid., p. 108.

of the latter. Not only does he contend that the language of Christian faith misrepresents the reality about which it speaks (e. g., the statement that "God sent His Son to die for sinners" involves an improper use of language), but he also contends that this confession of faith must be validated by being restated in the language of some particular ontology and being judged by its canons. In this way, Ogden radically secularizes Christianity, for he denies that we can claim a truth in Christian faith except insofar as it can be translated into and confirmed by a secular intellectus, the "right" philosophy. He concludes: "Thus, to make good the claim that myth can be true requires a prodigious philosophical undertaking. One must provide nothing less than that 'right' philosophy which is the essential prerequisite of any adequate theological construction."[10]

A fully adequate reply to Ogden would require a criticism of the enterprise of ontology per se. This issue will be discussed in a later chapter. Our purpose here will simply be to consider the idea of myth generally and the inadequacy of Ogden's conception of myth in particular. In this way, we shall understand why the proposal to demythologize the Christian faith is wrong. For (1) myth speaks about reality properly, without misrepresenting it, and (2) to claim that a mythical assertion is true does not require a restatement of this assertion in other, nonmythical terms. Once we understand why these two assertions are true, we shall also understand why the program of demythologizing is misconceived.

FEELING AND RELIGIOUS EXPERIENCE

4

The analysis of religion by modern theologians tends toward the following consensus: that an irreducible element in "true religion" is a certain affection, or feeling.[11] There are, of course, theological opponents of this position: e. g., Barth and Brunner. But these opponents do not propose an alternative interpretation of religious experience. Rather, they propose that theology should take an "objective revela-

---

[10] *Ibid.*, p. 119.
[11] Basic works forming this consensus are Jonathan Edwards, *A Treatise Concerning Religious Affections*, Friedrich Schleiermacher, *On Religion*, Wilhelm Herrmann, *The Communion of the Christian with God . . .*, Rudolf Otto, *The Idea of the Holy*, Stephan Strasser, *Das Gemüt*. For the history of this tradition see Leo Spitzer, *Classical and Christian Ideas of World Harmony*.

tion" as its primary object of study (e. g., the Bible or an historical tradition) rather than a "subjective experience."

Two replies must be made to these opponents. First, even a theology which is based on Scripture must finally attempt to characterize the state of consciousness by which we experience Scripture as revelation. And second, even if religious experience is essentially a feeling, it does not follow from this that it is subjective, indescribable, and incommunicable. For feeling in general is a perception and it has a certain cognitive dimension.

By "feeling in general," I mean the irreducible, enduring state of consciousness which underlies and pervades the multiplicity of particular emotions, passions, feelings, "feeling tones," etc. (There is no standard technical vocabulary.) These particular feelings always embody this principal feeling, or mood (*Stimmung*). I shall bracket from consideration these particular feelings and their relation to feeling in general, and focus on this principal feeling, which is constitutive of religious experience. By definition, the terms "feeling" and "affection" will be used hereafter to designate feeling in general.

The concept of feeling can be clarified by defining the object of feeling. The object of feeling is not like the object of seeing. That is, it is not something like a tree, which can be denoted and denumerated "an individual." Rather, the object of feeling is a totality, or a whole; and an act of feeling is the perception of a whole.[12] By a "whole" I mean approximately what some psychologists call a "Gestalt." By the perception of a whole, I mean the perception of that simple unit which is the context for a system of internal relations and individuals which are its parts. The theological tradition which defines religious experience as a feeling generally correlates this term with wholes—the proper "object" of feeling.

The defense of the claim that feeling is a genuine experience of reality depends upon the determination of a genuine object of feeling, i. e., wholes. And the defense of the reality of wholes is twofold: (1) that they are experienced, and (2) that they are simple and cannot, therefore, be conceived to be composites which result from the mental act of combining individuals.[13]

The fact that a whole is not composed of the terms it orders (since

---

[12] A defense of the distinction between individuals and wholes appears in the following chapter.

[13] We are bracketing "relations" from consideration since the notion of wholes can be attained through the contrast with individuals.

it orders them) is the reason why wholes cannot be perceived by *observation* or made known by *indication*. It is this essential impossibility of denoting or denumerating wholes that encourages the specious contention that wholes are not real. But that wholes are not perceivable by observation does not mean that they are unreal; rather, it means that they are not individuals. However, we can further explain the assertion that wholes can be perceived by specifying the perceptual characteristic of feeling.

5

Feeling perceives by participation. Just as feeling is a perception of a whole, so a whole is that which is perceived through participation. In the perception of a whole, the self takes up a position within the whole. In this respect, therefore, the perception of wholes differs from the perception of individuals, for individuals can be observed and denoted from "outside." In observation, the perceiver and that which is perceived are not one (that is, the former does not take up a position as "part" of the latter). Rather, they stand in opposition to each other. But in feeling, the perceiver is one with the thing perceived. Thus feeling is a simple kind of consciousness "which involves no analysis, comparison, or any process whatsoever . . ." (Peirce).[14]

The unity of the perceiver with a whole in the simple consciousness of feeling is not simply a participation, but a participation by affectional communion (a "feeling of wholeness"). In this affectional communion the subject is infused, or pervaded, with that which characterizes the whole (i. e., with something which, from another point of view, is not himself). For example, we feel "the immensity of the ocean" or "the presence of another." In these cases, "the ocean's immensity" and "the other's presence" seem to fill our consciousness so that we become one with them in affectional communion. This communion, or feeling of wholeness, is a sense of direct participation in the reality of another. Hence, it "is the original expression of an *immediate* existence-relationship" (Schleiermacher).[15]

Thomas Kelly, a profound modern mystic, isolates just these characteristics in his description of the feeling of the presence of God:

[14] *Collected Papers*, C. Hartshorne and P. Weiss, eds. (Cambridge, Mass., 1960), I, par. 306, p. 150.
[15] *Friedrich Schleiermachers sämmtliche Werke*, II/2, p. 586. Cited in Richard Niebuhr, *Schleiermacher on Christ and Religion* (New York, 1964), **p. 121.**

"The sense of Presence is as if two beings were joined in one single configuration, and the center of gravity is not in us but in that Other. As two bodies, closely attached together and whirling in the air, are predominantly determined by the heavier body, so does the sense of Presence carry within it a sense of our lives being in large part guided, dynamically moved from beyond our usual selves."[16]

Because the "felt-whole" affects a perceiver by uniting him with itself, it creates a context of perception. This context gives rise to two other feelings that accompany the feeling of wholeness. These are (1) the feeling of rightness ("fittingness"), and (2) the feeling of well-being ("happiness").[17] The feeling of rightness is a perception of the rightness in things in general. Through such a feeling we perceive that things are what they are because of a certain general required-ness, or rightness. This sense of rightness accompanies the feeling of wholeness because a whole determines a perspective from which certain individuals and relations that seemed at first to lack unity can now be perceived to be its parts. The sense of these individuals belonging to a whole involves the feeling of rightness by which we perceive that they harmonize, or consent to each other, to the whole, and to the perceiver who participates in the whole. Such a general feeling of rightness is manifested in the "Aha experience," when we discern the unity of a multiplicity of terms within a Gestalt. This is when "the penny drops."[18]

The feeling of wholeness is also accompanied by the feeling of well-being ("happiness"). Well-being, or happiness, is the feeling of being given what one wants, i. e., the feeling accompanying fulfillment.[19]

[16] Thomas Kelly, *A Testament of Devotion* (New York, 1941), p. 96.

[17] The distinction is traditional. For example, Anselm speaks of *rectitudo* and *commodum,* Edwards of excellency and happiness, Ross of the right and the good.

[18] Ian Ramsey uses this expression to indicate the moment of disclosure in a religious experience. The examples he gives are taken from Gestalt psychology. See *Religious Language* (New York, 1963), pp. 22-30.

[19] Happiness is, for example, when a little girl gets the doll she has "always wanted." She does not simply get a doll, she also gets a general sense that the world she lives in "cares" and will respond to her desires and her efforts. This sense of happiness is, therefore, a genuine feeling that life is successful. From such a feeling, a person is encouraged to try again, to move on. Abraham Maslow notes just this point when he writes: "Such experiences not only mean moving on, but have a feedback effect on the Self, in the feeling of certainty . . . self-trust, self-esteem." *Toward a Psychology of Being* (New York, 1962), p. 55. There are, in fact, certain "cosmic gifts" which engender a general sense of happiness; these are traditionally called "grace." Christianity should begin

When we are given what we want, we feel acknowledged by something more than ourselves. In a general feeling of well-being, we sense the tendency of all reality to fulfill what we desire and thereby to acknowledge our existence. When we have this feeling, we sense ourselves to be parts of a whole. The feeling of well-being, therefore, sustains self-esteem; and the lack of this feeling destroys it.

The feelings both of rightness and of well-being accompany the feeling of wholeness. Morever, these two feelings are inextricably bound up with each other. The feeling of well-being, or happiness, depends upon wanting what is right—since we can receive from the whole only what is present there, and what is present there is only what is right. The feeling of rightness depends upon the feeling of being acknowledged—since the rightness in things includes their fitting consent not only to each other and to the whole, but also to the perceiver, who is part of the whole by virtue of his affection toward it.[20] Hence, a felt-whole implies the presence of the feelings of wholeness, rightness, and well-being.

6

No states of consciousness are exclusively feeling experiences. Our conscious experience is complex, involving a fusion of feeling perceptions, sensible observations and symbolic relations. However, in certain experiences one or another of the aspects named above seems to predominate, e. g., "observation" or "participation." This is the case with religious experience. Therefore religious experience cannot be completely identified with the feeling perception it involves even if we acknowledge that this feeling seems to be the predominant element.

The definition of the feeling characteristic of religious experience is as follows. In religious experience, a person feels the All-encompassing Whole. Because this feeling involves the participation of the subject, it is an experience of being part of the life of God. Edwards described this experience as follows: ". . . there came into my soul,

---

talking about "grace" much more forthrightly than it has in modern times since this concept is essential to understanding moral and intellectual growth.

[20] From the metaphysical point of view, the feeling of rightness is the presupposition of the feeling of well-being; however, the two are so conjoined that they tend to be simultaneous in experience.

and was as it were diffused through it, a sense of the glory of the Divine Being; a new sense, quite different from any thing I ever experienced before. . . . I thought with myself, how excellent a Being that was, and how happy I should be, if I might enjoy that God, and be rapt up to him in heaven, and be as it were swallowed up in him forever!"[21]

Edwards' feeling of union with the All-encompassing Whole was accompanied by the two other feelings we have discussed. It included feelings of (1) the general rightness of all things ("how excellent a Being that was") and (2) well-being ("how happy I should be, if I might enjoy that God, and be rapt up to him in heaven"). The feeling of union, then, is not identical with the sense of judgment (rightness) nor with a sense of personal salvation (well-being), though it is accompanied by these two feelings, which are distinct, though secondary, perceptions of the whole.

From these considerations, we can understand why religious experience has a transforming power and converts the subject to a new form of life. For the affection produced in a man by his participation in the Whole redirects his sense of rightness and well-being. With regard to the psychological and epistemological structure of such an experience, there is no difference between the transforming and elevating power of a finite whole and that of the infinite Whole. Therefore aesthetic feeling and religious feeling are similar in kind, though caused by different objects and encompassing different ranges of life.

IMAGES OF THE FELT-WHOLE

7

Our discussion has already presupposed that myth is formally similar to such things as models, archetypes, metaphors, and icons. We have, in fact, suggested that the best term for designating this class of symbols is "image." Myths are images used in religion; ideal forms are images used in controlling social behavior; metaphors are images used in poetry; "brands" are images used in advertising. Myths, ideal types, metaphors, and brands all belong to the same class of symbols because they all have the same foundation in the psychic life of man and

---

[21] Jonathan Edwards, "Memoirs," *The Works of President Edwards* (New York, 1881), I, p. 16. Edwards' term "excellent" means "right." I have drawn heavily on Edwards's account of excellence in my description of rightness.

embody the content they symbolize in the same manner. All these images symbolize wholes—though myth symbolizes the All-encompassing Whole.

We must distinguish images from signs. Signs symbolize individuals; images symbolize wholes. Signs communicate by denotation, images by evocation. Signs are the means for communicating observations, images for communicating feeling experiences. Signs are external to the realities they signify (just as an observer is external to the object he observes); hence signs are conventional and replaceable. Images, on the other hand, participate in the reality they express (just as the subject participates in a whole by feeling); hence images are irreplaceable. Without an image, a feeling experience is not only incommunicable but lost forever. For if a feeling experience requires that its subject be included in and affected by the whole, then any phenomenally given whole is as transitory as the felt perception of it. Consider, for example, that moment when T. S. Eliot felt "the evening spread out against the sky as a patient etherized upon a table." That moment was a unique whole, which included Eliot's feeling of it. But without the poetic image it would be lost forever. Thus in speaking of images McLuhan rightly points out that "the medium is the message."[22]

The fact that the realities experienced in feeling are preserved only in images accounts for the fact that images communicate not by naming but by evoking the reality they express. They can evoke this reality from themselves because they are expressive forms of it. A sign is not the expressive form of the individual that it names; but an image is the expressive form of the whole that it evokes. If we may take seriously the report of poets and prophets, then this expressive form is "given" by a whole to its perceiver—for it is the whole that affects him. Hence, it is not inappropriate to say that the expressive symbol is *revealed* to the subject and he is *inspired* to receive it.[23] The act by which the poet or the prophet receives this revelation of

[22] *Op. cit.,* ch. 1.

[23] For example, Jacob Boehme's introductory sentences in his *Confessions* read as follows. "Art has not wrote this, neither was there any time to consider how to set it punctually down, according to a right understanding of letters, but all was ordered to the direction of the Spirit, which often went in haste; so that in many words letters may be wanting, and in some places a capital letter for a word. . . . I can write nothing of myself but as a child which neither knows nor understands anything, which neither has ever been learnt; and I write only that which the Lord vouchsafes to know in me according to the measure as himself manifests in me."

the whole in an expressive symbol is by the insight of his imagination. As such, imagination is the tongue of feeling, giving utterance to its perceptions. Such a view of imagination as a power of insight which receives the revelation of an expressive form is different from the popular notion of imagination as a sheer power of creation whereby man calls a fantasy-world into being. But I suggest that it is better able to account for the power of symbols to affect man and to transform and unify his life.

8

This account of the status of images is consistent with a number of statements about them in the contemporary theological and psychological "consensus."[24] (1) Images participate in the reality they symbolize, and this is why they evoke it rather than denote it. (2) Images seem to exist independently of man; they are born and they die, and we cannot create them at will. (3) Images have the power to affect the lives of persons and to transform and integrate (or disintegrate) them. (4) A special charisma is imputed to the creators and bearers of images and a special power to the images themselves.

This complex of statements about the character of images is consistent with the affirmation that images are revealed, or given, to man. But such revelation-and-insight takes place only at a determinate center. This center is the point from which the contextual whole is constituted, since it is here that the whole and the individuals and relations which are its parts can be seen to "intersect." This center, accordingly, provides access to the experience of the Whole. In religions, it is the "door" or "way" to life; it is the *kairos* or the *axis mundi*, ". . . the paradoxical place where [two worlds] communicate, where passage from the profane to the sacred world becomes possible" (sacred = Whole, profane = multiplicity of individuals).[25]

The first experience of the Whole from a given center is only possible for one who discovers himself at this center. This is the prophet, who finds himself caught up in the Whole and whose utterance expresses his concrete affection of it. Subsequent experiences of this Whole are possible for those who are affected by the prophet's

[24] For an example of such a "consensus" see the collection of essays in *Myth and Symbol,* F. Dillistone, ed. (London, 1965).

[25] Mircea Eliade, *The Sacred and the Profane,* W. Trask, trans. (New York, 1961), p. 25.

utterance and feel the Whole as he felt it. Thus a prophet's utterance docs not simply evoke the Whole, but evokes the Whole as experienced from a determinate center. It evokes a felt-whole. Gerhard Lenski describes this phenomenon from the sociological point of view as follows:

. . . the theologies of most contemporary religious groups are more than trivia generated by contact with the hard realities of the current social situation. Rather, they are in large measure a heritage from the past, and at the very least reflect the exposure of past generations of believers to the social environment of earlier eras. . . . From this we might suppose that the theology of any religious association is the accumulated residue of responses to the social environment, both past and present. This gives us a closer approximation to reality, but when we get down to cases we discover the problem is even more complicated. If, for example, we examine the theological heritage of contemporary Mormonism, we discover that while it reflects the influence of the frontier environment of nineteenth-century America, it reflects the influence of this environment *as it was experienced by Joseph Smith.* Whatever else we may say of Joseph Smith, he was no ordinary frontiersman of his day. Thus it is a matter of profound consequence that the environmental influences of the early nineteenth-century frontier on Mormonism were mediated through this unusual man.[26]

Lenski here describes the fact that the myths, or religious images, which always determine the character of a theology, do not symbolize a nude Whole, but a determinate felt-Whole. Hence, the image of the Whole mediates a felt-Whole, that is, the Whole as it is felt by a particular prophet. The prophet cannot, therefore, be separated from the religious image, since this myth necessarily implies his mediatorial position at the *axis mundi.* This explains the peculiar authoritative status of founders of religions. It explains why, for example, there can be no Christianity without Jesus Christ, no Mormonism without Joseph Smith, no Judaism without Moses. And it explains why we can experience the Whole of which a prophet speaks only by joining him at the *axis mundi* and entering into his feeling of it. Thus, for example, Christianity asserts that we can experience the Whole only as we "take up the cross" and put on "the mind that was in Christ Jesus." Christian experience presupposes, therefore, the affirmation of Jesus Christ in His mediatorial office.

[26] Gerhard Lenski, *The Religious Factor* (New York, 1963), p. 337 f.

9

Because images evoke a felt-whole, they move the subject to a determinate center from which that whole appears. That is, they create a specific feeling in a person. This means there is a genuine difference in religious experience from one religion to another. It is not correct to say that men who use different religious images all have the same religious feeling. For since a religious image evokes not the Whole, but a determinate felt-Whole, differences in religious images imply differences both in the feeling of wholeness and in the felt-Wholes themselves. Hence, discernible differences in piety, spirituality, and feeling of virtue provide a basis for discriminating religions from one another with regard to their experience of God.

Moreover, the difference in religious images from religion to religion implies that the feeling of a religious community will not be merely the general sense of wholeness, rightness, and well-being. Rather, this general feeling will be expressed in determinate "modal feelings" which are appropriate to a given religious symbol-complex. In Christianity, the modal feelings "of faith, hope, and love are formed in the soul by the Christological symbol-complex (i. e., by the sacraments and liturgy, by prayer and the reading of Scripture, and by the community ethos). Whereas all religions include the general feelings of wholeness, rightness, and well-being—since these three feelings characterize every sense of the Whole—religions will differ with respect to the modal feelings through which this general feeling is manifested.[27]

Religions are, in part, communities that are created and sustained by myths that form habitual modal feelings in the lives of their members. These habitual modal feelings are one of the bases for a religious communion among persons. While there may be private religious feeling which is not expressed in images, there can be no shared religious feeling without the use of religious images, or myths. The religious symbol-complex which is able to evoke the felt-Whole is the vehicle for the communication of religious feeling and the principle, thereafter, of continuing religious communion.

[27] By acknowledging that all religions involve the same three general feelings, but recognizing that these general feelings are manifested through different modal feelings, we can account both for the similarities and the differences that are found in various religions, their myths, their rites, their moral codes, etc.

THE "STORY" LEVEL OF MEANING

10

A primary vehicle of religious communication is myth, a linguistic image that evokes the All-encompassing Whole. As with poetry, the mythic story contains the reality it evokes within itself. "The medium is the message." Hence, a specific religious experience is inextricably bound up with a specific myth, a "story-image."

Since the mythical medium is the message, the kind of demythologizing procedure that Ogden calls for is impossible—for Ogden requires that we state the meaning of a mythical affirmation "in other nonmythical terms." This presupposes that the message of myth exists outside the myth rather than within it. It presupposes that myths communicate by referring rather than evoking. It presupposes that myths are signs rather than images. Ogden says as much: ". . . myth refers to a certain language or form of speaking which, like other languages, functions to represent (to *re*-present, to present *again*) some field of experience in a particular way."[28]

Ogden contends that "human experience has different fields and that this is reflected in our (logically) different languages."[29] I agree with this judgment and have tried to show how there are differences in language (though not "different languages"). I have shown not only how signs and images are related to different fields of experience, but also how they function differently in communication. What is striking about Ogden's view, on the other hand, is that he violates his own principle. Rather than showing how mythical discourse and scientific discourse function differently, he actually asserts that both these languages function in the same way. He holds that both these "languages" function by signifying, or "*re*-presenting," an independent datum of experience. In this decisive respect, Ogden holds that myth is not different from but is "like other languages." The logical rules appropriate to signification govern both mythical discourse and scientific discourse alike. In what respect, then, are these two kinds of discourse *logically different*?

Ogden attempts to explain the difference between mythical discourse and scientific discourse by asserting that myth *re*-presents

[28] *Op. cit.*, p. 104.
[29] *Ibid.*

"inner awareness" by mis*re*-presenting it—since myth uses terms and
categories derived from our "external perception of reality as the
object of our ordinary sense perception."[30] But it does not seem that
"misrepresenting" can be the criterion for distinguishing a "logically"
different language. For then the misrepresentation of physical objects
by a scientific statement could be claimed to be not an error, but only
"another way of speaking." Ogden is driven to this odd account of the
difference between mythical discourse and scientific discourse because
of the error of his original assumption. That is, he assumes that both
mythical discourse and scientific discourse gain their meaning by
signifying *something else:* the former *signifies* something in "inner
awareness," the latter *signifies* something in "external awareness."
Hence the difference between them must be accounted for as a difference in the way these two kinds of language signify, or represent, a
datum of experience. From this false assumption, Ogden then derives
his assertion that mythical language signifies in a false way, i. e., by
misrepresenting the object to which it refers. If he had differentiated
mythical speaking from scientific speaking in terms of other criteria, he might have shown that there is a logical difference between
these two kinds of language. Mythical discourse utilizes images in
order to evoke a feeling of the whole; hence, mythical discourse must
conform to the logic of wholes. Scientific description utilizes signs in
order to represent individuals; hence, scientific descriptions must conform to the logic of signification.

11

Because myth functions as an image which evokes rather than as a
sign which *re*-presents, the meaning of mythical discourse does not
arise at the sign-level, i. e., at the level of signification. Rather, the
meaning of mythical discourse arises at the level of the total story,
the most complex unit of linguistic utterance. The linguistic unit
appropriate to myth is not the single word nor even the sentence, but
the story. We frequently assert that myths are stories, but fail to
consider what this fact implies for the meaning of myth. Let us turn
to this problem.

Language is not simply a collection of naming words. Rather it
is a complex unity where naming words are joined into sentences,
which are joined into paragraphs, which are joined into stories. Each

[30] *Ibid.*

of these linguistic units involves a different function of language and a different level of meaning. The meaning of a naming word comes from the thing it signifies. For this reason, naming words are conventional, replaceable signs. The word "man" can be replaced by the word "homme" without any difference in meaning, because both words draw their meaning from the object which they signify.

The meaning of a sentence, on the other hand, involves something more than the meaning of all the naming words it contains. "Sentential meaning" occurs on a different level from that of naming, or signifying. Sentences unite naming words by using symbols that perform certain operations upon, or establish certain relations among, these naming words. Sentences are created by employing such syntactical operators as "but," "whether," "and," "not," "unimportant," "greater than," and so forth. Note that these words are not naming words; their meaning does not depend upon a sensible perception of either the external world or inner *self*-consciousness. Ogden does not even consider such syntactical operators, or their function in establishing a meaning level which is more than "*re*-presenting" or signifying. He evidently assumes that the meaning of all language arises in the course of naming something else. But what kind of something else do "but" or "whether" represent?

Ogden might attempt to counter this criticism by admitting that syntactical operators add something to naming words, but denying that there is any independent meaning in a sentence apart from its particular naming words. Yet this is not the case. By symbolic logic we can show that there is a meaning in sentence patterns alone, and that this meaning is completely independent of the naming words a particular sentence contains. Jerome Bruner, the Harvard psychologist, provides an elegant illustration of this point. Suppose, he says, we give children the following table:

1	2	3	4	5
The	man	ate	his	lunch
A	lady	wore	my	hat
This	doctor	broke	a	bottle
My	son	drove	our	car

The children "soon discover that so long as they pick words in the order 1 2 3 4 5, from any place in each column, something 'sensible' can be got: even if it is silly or not true, like 'My doctor wore a car'

F

or 'A lady ate a bottle,' it is at least not 'crazy' like 'Man the lunch his ate.' "[31] This experiment shows that sentences have a meaning that is independent of the naming words they contain. Sentences may be "sensible" or meaningful on one level even if they are "silly" or not true on another. The same thing holds for mythical stories.

By discerning the different levels of meaning in language, we can appreciate the deficiency in Ogden's conception of mythical discourse. He never suggests that the meaning of a mythical discourse might occur on any other level than that appropriate to a naming word. Consider his examples of myth-like utterances: "Oxford University," "the Lord is an everlasting rock," "the divine creation of the world," "personal God," and others.[32] These examples suggest that he thinks of a myth as "naming language" which acquires its meaning from that to which it *refers* and which it misrepresents. But the linguistic unit appropriate to mythical utterance is not a naming word. For example, the disciples did not run about shouting "Resurrection! Resurrection!" Rather, they preached a religious discourse; they told a story about the alpha and omega of life. And just as the meaning of a sentence is more than that of all the naming words it contains, so the meaning of every story is more than that of all the sentences it contains. Thus we arrive at a third level of linguistic meaning, a level twice-removed from that of simple signification.

12

We can understand the kind of meaning appropriate to stories by considering the following example. When children are in the first and second grades, they are given paragraph-long stories to read and are asked to suggest appropriate titles. They reply with a word or a phrase or a sentence: "Johnny takes a trip," "A surprise for Ruth," "Pirate Paul and the sunken ship," and so on. The purpose of this exercise is to help the children grasp the meaning of the story as a whole. They are asked to see its "point." In so doing, they come to understand how the meaning of the story is more than the meaning of all the words and all the sentences it contains. They show that they see the meaning of the story by summarizing it in a title, which is an image of the story taken as a whole. To utter this title, or image, evokes the whole story.

[31] Jerome Bruner, *Toward a Theory of Instruction* (Cambridge, Mass., 1966), p. 78 f.
[32] Ogden, *op. cit.*, pp. 105-107, 118.

Suppose, however, that someone fails to understand the utterance "Johnny takes a trip" as the summary title, or image, of an entire story. Suppose someone thinks this sentence to be a descriptive assertion which refers to one denumerable event among many. In this case, he would simply misunderstand the image, for he would have interpreted it to be a sign. This is exactly the kind of confusion that bedevils Ogden's understanding of myth, and such a confusion is not confined to him alone. Many, perhaps most, contemporary Protestant theologians make this same mistake when they understand the Christian affirmation "The meaning of the Scriptures is the crucifixion and resurrection of Jesus Christ" to be a descriptive assertion, or an historical statement referring to a single event. This mistake leads them to affirm that the Scripture is not revelation, but is only a "witness" to the "Christ-event"—the true revelation. But this conclusion is not correct. It misunderstands the meaning of the confession that the Scriptures are "about" Jesus Christ. It thinks that this confession is a descriptive assertion which signifies an historical event that can be separated out from Scripture itself and set in opposition to other events in its story.

The Christian confession that the meaning of Scripture is Jesus Christ must be understood as a title, or image, that intends to evoke the meaning of the whole. That is why Jesus Christ cannot be separated from Scripture and set over against it. He is only a shorthand way of expressing "the instant vision of a complex process that ordinarily extends over a long period."[33] To discover such an image or title that expresses the unity of a complex story is to discover a meaning-structure as unique and irreducible as the meaning-structure Bruner showed to exist in individual sentence patterns. With respect to its own level of meaning, myth speaks properly. Moreover, it cannot be reduced to, or reexpressed in, some other form of language.

13

Ogden's assertion that myth must be validated by reexpressing its meaning in other, nonmythical language can now be seen to rest on a false conception of the terms of the problem. The reality that myth symbolizes is evoked by the myth itself and cannot be experienced apart from it. Hence, the truth of a mythical discourse consists solely in its power of illumination, or its ability to create feelings of whole-

---

[33] McLuhan, *op. cit.*, p. 25.

ness, rightness, and well-being in a person.[34] In producing these affections, a myth validates itself—just as Scripture validates itself when it creates a new sense of the meaning of life in the Christian. Thus myths are validated by experience, just as descriptions are validated by experience; but both are validated by different kinds of experience.

The truth of myth is not the only kind of truth, nor are the criteria of mythical truth the criteria of all truth. The test of the truth of symbolic sentence patterns is, for example, rational consistency. The test of the truth of descriptions is a correspondence between a sign and the thing it signifies. Moreover, there are tests for discriminating different kinds of utterance from each other and thereby determining the test, or tests, of truth appropriate in each case. Further, each kind of truth puts a certain demand on the others.

By enumerating these other aspects of truth, we make clear that our definition of mythical truth as the evocation of the feelings of wholeness, rightness, and well-being does not exhaust the notion of truth per se. Moreover, our definition of mythical truth does not impugn the rational and empirical criteria appropriate to the various intellectual disciplines. The sole intellectual discipline that is rendered impossible by our analysis is the kind of philosophical ontology to which Ogden is committed. Whether it is possible to develop a metaphysics that forthrightly acknowledges the mythic dimension of reality without also depreciating other aspects of experience is a problem we shall take up in the following essay.

[34] The implicit reference to Augustine's theory of illumination is intended. Cf. ch. 4, sec. 9c. The general similarity between the kind of experience I have been describing and Maslow's "peak experiences" is striking. See *Toward a Psychology of Being*, esp. ch. 6.

IV

A Philosophy of Unity[*]

METACRITICISM

1. *Metacriticism and Henology*

The distinguishing trait of twentieth-century intellectual life is the emergence and proliferation of the "meta-disciplines" (or "meta-sciences"): e.g., meta-mathematics, meta-logic, meta-ethics, meta-jurisprudence, meta-politics, meta-theater, meta-language (hermeneutics and linguistic analysis), meta-sociology (sociology of knowledge), and so on.[1] The emergence of these meta-disciplines signifies a fundamental change in human orientation. We may compare this contemporary movement with the development in the eighteenth and nineteenth centuries of the special sciences as self-contained disciplines: chemistry, biology, botany, geology, history, psychology, and so forth. Whereas this earlier period proliferated special sciences through the application of rigorous techniques which critically reduced (and therefore multiplied) the objects of science per se, the characteristic of contemporary intellectual life is the proliferation of

[1] Examples of contemporary metacriticism can be seen in the work of Firth (meta-ethics), Gadamer, deWaehlens (meta-language), Russell and Whitehead (meta-mathematics), White (meta-history), Söhngen (meta-jurisprudence), Scheler (meta-sociology), Abel (meta-theater), and Duméry (henological theory).

[*] "A Philosophy of Unity" originally appeared in a slightly different version in *Harvard Theological Review* 60 (1967), pp. 1-38. Copyright © 1967 by the President and Fellows of Harvard College. Reprinted by permission.

meta-disciplines through the critical analysis of the methods and presuppositions of the special sciences themselves. I believe this peculiar intellectual activity, which underlies the emergence of all contemporary meta-disciplines, is the major clue to understanding the fundamental reorientation of personal and social consciousness that is going on today. Moreover, this change is rich with possibilities for new ways of dealing with the technological and institutional problems of contemporary society.

My thesis does not, obviously, rest on any quantitative evidence, but upon an historical understanding of the development of its major terms, together with a formal analysis of the kinds of issues involved in contemporary intellectual life. Because of this historical perspective, I regard the emergence of various forms of metacriticism as the first fruits of a later, greater harvest. And if my thesis is correct, then it is of utmost importance not only to the intellectual but also to the social order. For just as the idea of "scientific man" suggested certain historical possibilities and limitations to one age, so the idea of "metacritical man" will come to suggest new possibilities and limitations for the future.[2]

The separation of the meta-disciplines from the special sciences presupposes a new distinction in the theoretical realm which is only beginning to be recognized and systematically considered. This is the distinction between "knowledge and reality" on the one hand and "unity" on the other. The study and theory of this latter term, unity, is called henology (theory of "the one").[3] As the theory of unity, henology is both distinct from, and the principle of, every method. Hence, metacriticism and the emergence of the meta-disciplines bring us to an explicit awareness of the henological problem.

The henological question has grown out of the process of development of the special sciences toward the meta-sciences. For the special sciences are distinguished by the critical reduction of their objects, and they depend upon rigorous artificial methods both for this critical discrimination of these objects and for their technical manipulation. Until recently the special sciences were pervaded by a "myth" which gave them their drive toward proliferation and organization during the

---

[2] For example, the suggestive power of McLuhan's studies on the difference between "print man" and "electronic man."

[3] I follow Duméry's "henology" rather than Gilson's "énology." For the contrast between ontology and henology see Henry Duméry, *The Problem of God in Philosophy of Religion,* C. Courtney, trans. (Evanston, Ill., 1964), esp, chap. 3.

period of their development: this was the conviction that the method peculiar to one special science ought also to be normative for others. Such an idea led to theories about a hierarchy of special sciences precisely because it failed to see the (legitimate) artificiality of the methods of these very sciences.

Today the growing awareness of the fact that the methods and unitizing principles governing the special sciences must be as much an object of our understanding and choice as the subjects they study is the condition that makes metacriticism possible. For metacriticism is based on the awareness that not only are the objects of science open to critical reduction and free selection (i. e., we can choose and control our object of study), but also the methods of dealing with these objects. Metacriticism opens up a freedom with regard to methods because it is the discipline which is concerned to elaborate the range of epistemological—and hence methodological—possibilities open to us.

Whereas the emergence of the special sciences depended upon the explicit development of new category systems, theories of explanation, and methodological precision, the development of the meta-sciences is dependent upon an explicit understanding of that unitizing principle which makes a multiplicity of category systems, modes of explanation, and methods possible. To understand this unitizing principle, and the complexity of the term "unity," is the task of henology. Just as the scientific discrimination of an object rests upon a precise method, so the meta-scientific discrimination of a method rests upon a precise notion of unity. Hence, only an exact theory of unity, or henology, makes a precise metacriticism possible. The special sciences rest on the distinction between subject matter and method; the meta-sciences rest on the distinction between method and unity (or the unitizing principle of that method). Henology is the study of unity as the principle of all methodological possibilities.

We may express roughly the same point in terms of a popular historical typology. It is commonly said that the emergence of the special sciences occurred when the epistemological problem was separated from the ontological problem and made prior to it; so, too, the meta-sciences are now emerging as the henological problem is separated from the epistemological problem and made prior to it. Hence, henology is the discipline which must be elaborated for us to gain a full understanding and free choice over the range of methodological possibilities open to us.

2. *Metacriticism and Sociotechnics*

Metacriticism is not the only tendency in contemporary thought. There is another, almost as strong, which seems to be its friend (since it also believes that the era of "scientific man" is drawing to an end), but is really its enemy (for metacriticism regards the special sciences and technology as a major value to be preserved). This contemporary anticriticism is characterized by its opposition to specialized knowledge in the name of intellectual synthesis, its opposition to sociotechnical procedures (e. g., computers and psychological testing) in the name of the "human values," and its depreciation of vocational specialization in the name of the "whole man." The consistent extension of this attitude into the social order is manifested in the preference for face-to-face relations, small neighborhoods, and organic (often hierarchical) society. But the problem with this anticritical philosophy is that there seems to be no way to attain its intellectual and social goals without either dispersing the apparatus of modern science or organically ordering it by a benevolent totalitarianism. Hence many modern social critics depreciate the intellectual and social institutions of technological civilization in the course of affirming the value of "general knowledge" and "person-to-person relations."

However, I believe there is no way to return to the society of the generalist or to reconstruct knowledge on his plan. By another analysis, however, we can see an alternative possibility for change. The alternative to the anticritical principle on the theoretical level is metacriticism and henology; for by henology we are able to elaborate a theory of methodological unity which justifies and integrates the very differentiation of knowledge and methods that the anticritical view opposes. The alternative to the anticritical principal on the social level is that institution whose sole concern is with the unification of the many specialized activities of sociotechnical civilization: management. Management is the institutional equivalent of theoretical henology. The work of management is to oversee the unity of the many specialized social functions, and its object is solely the organization of these functions and not their operation. Hence management is not a political function in the classical sense; for whereas politics, business, and teaching are arts, management is a meta-art.

Management and its instruments (e. g., testing, communications, computers) offer an institutional alternative both to the dispersion of technology and to the belief that technological sociey is a self-adjusting mechanism. Henology, the theoretical parallel to management, is specifically concerned to formulate those principles in terms of which managerial values are recognized and decision-making procedures established. Henology therefore provides the theoretical basis from which the full number of methodological possibilities can be understood and freely selected. In the remainder of this chapter I shall outline a philosophical henology.

IDENTITY AND EXISTENCE

3. *The Distinction Between Existence and Essence*[4]

The fundamental work of thought is to distinguish clearly between what things are and the fact that they are. The failure to make this distinction leads to the misunderstanding of existence as some determinate characteristic of some things by which they are distinguished from other things. So, for example, Plato proposed that the form persisting through all change is the being of a thing. But this was to confuse a kind of being with being itself, for there is no reason to assume that characteristics which persist are real while those which do not are not. A second example: Jonathan Edwards affirmed that whatever "consents" really exists and the more it is "consenting" the more real it is. Conversely, whatever does not "consent" at all *is not*. But Edwards' argument rests upon the fundamental category-mistake of all ontology, i. e., upon the confusion of a kind of being with the fact of being. A third example: Bergson affirmed that the characteristic of being is process, and process is prior to all particular differentiations. From this assertion he argued that intuition is superior to knowledge (which deals with differentiations). But Bergson simply reverses the position of Plato, without in any way overcoming the category-mistake implicit in his formulation, namely, the assumption that because something is of a certain kind, it has a greater tendency to be. This confusion of essence with existence is the fundamental category-mistake of all ontology.

By "essence" I mean any categorical determination that may be

---

[4] In this essay the terms "being" and "existence" will be used interchangeably. This usage will be justified by the position developed in the course of the essay.

predicated of two or more beings in the same respect. I include under this general definition all intellectual forms, all volitional motions, and all affectional moods. For example, not only is an "idea" an essence, but so is a "choice." And not only is a "mathematical relation" an essence, but so is any modal feeling—such as sadness or anxiety. Moreover, the concept of essence includes not only particular motions of the several abilities of mind, and their appropriate objects, but also the general term which designates all the particular motions appropriate to any one of these abilities. For example, not simply ideas, but also "understanding" is an essence; not only determinate choices, but also "volition" is an essence; not only particular moods, but also "feeling" is an essence.

4. The Universality of Being

The fundamental category-mistake is to equate existence with an essence. This is a mistake because there is no reason for thinking that one categorical determination should be hypostatized as the principle of the others. Why, for example, should we think that the immutable, by virtue of its immutability alone, is more real than the mutable? Or why should we think that "act," by virtue of its act-character alone, is the principle of every other categorical determination? Claims such as these are either meaningless or false, for there is no *reason* for thinking that any essence is more real than any other essence. Rather, since being cannot be equated with any essence, we must conceive it to be absolutely universal. It must encompass all that we experience. Considered in this respect, we call it "being in general." But now we must consider several proposals respecting the meaning of this term.

(1) Many philosophers argue that since "being in general" includes everything and excludes nothing, it is meaningless. It means nothing; it is merely a word. If this argument is correct then metaphysics is impossible, for metaphysics is the discipline which purports to take being qua being as its object of study. (2) But Hegel argued that from the fact that being does not delimit or signify any particular thing we should not conclude that being is meaningless; rather, we should conclude that being is absolutely indeterminate. He acknowledges that what is absolutely indeterminate is nothing, but asserts that, for the same reason, nothing is also being. In this way, Hegel rejects the logical principles of identity and noncontradiction. For if being is nothing and nothing is being, then everything is its contrary. According to

Hegel, the unification of these two contraries comes through something still more fundamental, namely, *becoming*. In becoming, being is united with its contrary; hence the process of becoming is governed by the principle of contradiction. (3) However, Tillich argues that the universality of being in general (Being Itself) does not mean that it is indeterminate and nothing; rather, it means that being is no particular thing. Being is something, though its ontological status is different from that of particular things: being "is," but particular things "exist." By distinguishing the notion of being from that of existence, Tillich maintains being's universality, unity, and reality. (4) The difficulty raised by Tillich's argument is that it separates the "really real" from that which we commonly experience—for "Being Itself" is absolutely transcendent. For this reason, Tillich's view generates a skepticism regarding the validity and value of our ordinary experience (though a less radical skepticism than mysticism). All philosophers who appeal to human experience as the criterion of truth and goodness will reject his position. Some will conclude that the notion of being is excluded by the criterion of experience, but others may follow William James in maintaining that experience does not exclude being, but only the claim that being is one. For if we impute reality (being) to everything in our experience, then being will be universal and real, but it will also be as plural as the number of distinctions we experience. (5) The pluralistic conception of being suggests, however, still another possibility, namely, that of Plotinus. Plotinus acknowledges that being is as plural as the number of distinctions in experience, but he goes on to distinguish the plurality of being from the unity of another hypostasis, the One. For even if we grant that being is plural, it may still have an underlying unity. The strength of Plotinus' solution is that it maintains the reality (being) of all that we experience. Essences are not mere appearance; they are real. But the cost of preserving the appearances in this way is to separate the world from its unity. For the One so transcends being that it cannot be known, but only communed with in a mystical manner.[5]

Had Plotinus made a more radical criticism of being in order to see that its plurality is the very mode of its unity, then he could have over-

[5] For the Greeks (and Plotinus) "one" was not strictly a number, but was the means by which all other numbers were defined and generated. This conception of "one" is related to the fact that the Greeks also did not understand zero, or "nothing," to be a number. The modern "positional" notion of zero came into Europe from the Arabic world, and it made possible a reunderstanding of "one" as a number beside other numbers.

come the deficiencies of his dichotomous system. But he was doomed to fail because he did not possess an adequate notion of unity. In what follows, therefore, we shall accept Plotinus' original insight that metaphysics should be developed henologically rather than ontologically (i. e., through the notion of unity rather than through the notion of being), but we shall develop this insight in a different way.

5. *That Being Is Unity*

When we speak of the being (existence) of a thing, we mean its unity. And we distinguish the unity of a thing from its essence, for we say that all existents are the same with respect to their being one and yet that they may be different with respect to their being whatever they are. Hence, it is possible to distinguish the unity of a thing from its essence.

Moreover, to define existence as unity makes it possible to understand how we can have an experience of existence. For in order to experience anything at all, we must grasp both its oneness and the essential determination of that oneness. This oneness of a thing appears to be nothing other than its being, since this unity is what we mean when we refer to *that* thing—whether it be *"that* horse," *"an* equation," or *"the* universe."

In later scholastic philosophy the technical terms *haecceitas* ("thatness") and *quidditas* ("whatness") could be used to distinguish existence from essence. This is the distinction I am appropriating in order to define being as unity. For insofar as we refer to the thatness of a thing, we refer to its oneness, i. e., to the fact that it exists. In so doing, we are affirming not only that existence (being) is unity, but that it is only unity. For we can neither think nor experience anything at all unless it is one, and we can neither think nor experience the being of anything to be something more than its oneness. Hence, being is unity and only unity. (This does not mean, of course, that we cannot continue to use the word "being," but it only clarifies what this word means. This clarification allows us to note, however, that the existential and predicative uses of the term "is" have unity in common: the existential use of the term refers to a unit, and the predicative use of the term signifies a unition.)

Within the tradition of western philosophy, it is Thomas Aquinas who has come the closest to formulating the insight that being is unity. But he did not develop the consistent henology that I am proposing.

For although Thomas asserts that ". . . *ens et unum convertuntur*" ("being and one are interchangeable"), he does not elevate this assertion to the first principle of his metaphysics.[6] For Thomas holds that *ens* is a being which is the unity of an essence and an act of existence (*esse*). Hence, *ens* is not identical with *esse* (pure act); and it is *esse* which is Thomas's true metaphysical principle. Were I arguing the issue in these terms, I would maintain that oneness and *esse* (existence) are interchangeable notions. Thus my position is not the same as Thomas', although it is consistent with his insights into the henological principle *"ens et unum."*

The view of Thomas is not a consistent henology, for by elevating the "pure act" of *esse* into his metaphysical principle he not only makes the category-mistake which is at the basis of every ontology, but is also forced to deny that the ultimate principle of all things is itself any denumerable "one." For although Thomas holds that everything that exists is one, yet that which is ultimate is not properly called "one" since it is not properly said to exist. (". . . *non possumus dicere quod ipsum esse sit.*")[7] He seems to hold that *ens et unum convertuntur* when (and only when) the *unum* is an individual. So, too, the oneness of number cannot be an *unum* which is interchangeable with being, although this oneness of number is really one. (Thomas writes: ". . . *unum dupliciter dicitur. Est enim unum quod convertitur cum ente, et est unum quod est principium numeri.*")[8] But the view which I am proposing is not only that *ens et unum* are interchangeable, but also that every "one" is a being. Hence, although I agree with Thomas that every individual is real and is one, I disagree with him by maintaining that relations and wholes are real and are one, and are real because they are one. Thus, as we shall see, even the *unum quod est principium numeri* should be affirmed to exist.

6. *That Unity Is Identity*

The affirmation that being is unity accounts not simply for the oneness of things, but also for their "resistance," or "facticity." For my argument does not intend to indicate that unity is a purely formal

[6] Thomas Aquinas, *Quaestiones quodlibetales,* Quod. VI, q. 1, a. 1.

[7] Thomas Aquinas, *Exposition in librum Boethii de hebdomadibus,* II.

[8] Thomas Aquinas, *Scriptum super libros sententiarum magistri Petri Lombardi,* Lib. I, d. 24, q. 1, a. 1.

mode by which all things are conceived. Rather, I wish to argue that unity is "in" all things because it is, in fact, the "power," "force," "facticity," and "hardness" of their being. Unless we can account for this existential character of being, we cannot claim that being is unity. The argument I propose is as follows. The unity of a thing is the unity of a determinate essence, and this unity considered as the unity of that essence is nothing other than what we call an *identity*. For the identity of a thing is *that whatness*. The thatness of things is their oneness; but this oneness is their identity, or the fact that, *whatever* they are, they are *that* thing, and they are irreducibly that thing. The oneness, or identity, of a thing makes it *that* thing and preserves it from being another thing or no thing at all. All things, however they may differ one from another, are always *those* (that and that and that, etc.) things. *Identity* is common to them all; it is "one" in them all. For however different things are with respect to essence, they are always the same in that they are identities, or *ones*. Each and every thing has a determinate identity, and its identity is its existential oneness.

From the notion of unity as identity, we are able to deal with the question about the hardness, or force, or resistance which many philosophers have taken to be the determinate characteristic of being. For it seems that identity is nothing other than the determinate oneness of things by which they resist becoming what they are not, or resist becoming nothing at all. This gives them their hardness, or facticity. We might argue for this position in the following ways: (1) we might show that the root meaning of the term "identity" expresses an experience of the thatness of a thing whereby it endures and remains the same (*idem*); (2) we might advert to the various phenomenological reductions of philosophers, wherein they note that the being of things is nothing other than their force, or their resistance to becoming other than they are, or their power to remain irreducibly one (e. g., Edwards's atoms); and (3) we might approach the problem of identity by means of metaphysical analysis and classificaion. But in each of these three approaches to the being of things we would see that the force or power we find in them is the consequence of their being determinate identities, or "ones." Therefore, our thesis that the being of things is their oneness is adequate to account not only for the more formal problems of metaphysics but also for the primary experience of being as a power of resistance.

7. The Principles of Logic Established in Being Itself

We can now understand the maxim that essence and existence are not two separate objects, nor are they to be relegated to two separate realms of experience. For since the existence of a thing is nothing other than the identity or oneness of whatever that thing is, then to know the being of a thing is simply to know that thing itself. It is not the case that there is one knowledge of the thatness (oneness) of a thing and another knowledge of its whatness; rather, every knowledge of a thing is a single knowledge of its essence and existence, or its whatness and its oneness. For this reason, the knowledge of existence is one with the knowledge of essence, even though this one knowledge can be distinguished by reflection into that which is the same in all things (their being, identity, or oneness) and that which differs from thing to thing (their whatness or essence). Moreover, this accounts for the fact that existence cannot be understood apart from an essence, for it is the oneness of that essence, i. e., its identity. And it accounts for the fact that essence cannot be understood apart from existence because if the unity of an essence were removed from it, it could no longer be what it is.

By this argument, we overcome the deficiencies of philosophies which regard essence and existence as two separate objects of knowledge. For example, it might be suggested that we can have (1) a knowledge of essences as not-existing and (2) a knowledge of essences as existing and (3) an idea of existence per se (Being Itself). But this separation of essence and existence into separate objects of knowledge is just another form (although a more sophisticated form) of the fundamental category-mistake. For in order for a nonexistent essence to be a distinct object of knowledge, it must have a surreptitious kind of existence; and in order for existence to be a separate object of knowledge, it must have a surreptitious kind of essence. For only a *what* can be known, and we can know a what only because it is *that* what. So we see that essence and existence cannot ever be separated into two objects of knowledge, and we can never speak of them as if they were ever found apart from each other. From this fact that essence and existence are always found together in a single object, we see that the being that characterizes each thing is its identity, or unity.

From this it follows that the fundamental principles of logic **are,** in fact, expressions of existence. For existence is nothing other than the unity which we call identity; and the *principle of identity,* and those principles and combinations which necessarily follow from it and reexpress it, provide a description of what is in fact the case.

THREE CATEGORY SYSTEMS

8. *The Three Hypostases of Unity*

By asserting that being is that oneness which constitutes the identity of things, we are able to give an account of being which maintains its universality without either (1) relegating it to a transcendent order or (2) sacrificing its intrinsic unity. For even though being is as multiple as those objects which can be identified (trees, chimeras, algebraic relations, the universe, etc.), still it is as unified as the notion of identity itself. *However, it is not the case that there is only one kind of identity.* For unity is a complex notion, and the recognition of this fact allows us to account for certain traditional difficulties confronting philosophical analysis. Moreover, it is precisely because unity is a complex notion that we can generate a multiplicity of ways to unitize, categorize, and explain, and it is this possibility of generating different ways to unitize and categorize that is at the basis of the new metacritical sciences.

We can attain to an inclusive notion of the distinctions appropriate to unity in two ways. (1) We may engage in a direct henological analysis of this term, so that by the examination of unity per se we attain to an idea of its various forms, or hypostases—since the various kinds of unity are not simply modes of another unity which is prior to them but are each determinate existences of the One. (2) We may analyze the various concepts of "simple being" implied in the various category-systems that have been developed in the history of thought. We shall consider this problem from both vantage points.

By direct henological analysis, we can attain to the conclusion that the unity of everything that exists is (1) the unity of any denumerable individual, or *individuality,* or (2) the unity of any two or more individuals when taken together, or considered as one thing—i. e., *relationality,* or (3) the unity of any, or all, possible relationalities considered as complete, or *wholeness.* It should be noted that no one of these terms is either more or less one than the others. For this reason, even though the second and third kinds of unity may include the first, the first neither exists from them nor they from it. Therefore, the unity characteristic of relationality does not subsume, or necessarily include, the individuals which it relates. It is a simple which is capable of uniting (or unites) two terms. But the distinctiveness of the terms united remains even after they are related, and the relation is an object in its own right whether or not its terms are existing individuals (e. g., they may simply be relational intersections). So, for example, the object "five feet" is the same whether its two terms are individual men, or whether its terms are not individuals at all, but relational intersections. This is why we can speak of a relation as either uniting, or being capable of uniting, individuals; and it is why we may consider relations as objects in themselves. (Thus, the possibility of symbolic logic.) Still further, this explains why "a possible world" has, from the standpoint of pure relationality, as much reality as anything else in the real world. For, from the point of view of relationality, a thing is real if it can be expressed or experienced as a determinate relation. Hence, I agree with W. James that "the relations that connect experiences must themselves be experienced relations, and any kind of relation experienced must be accounted as real as anything else in the system."[9]

In the same way, we may note that a whole designates a simple and distinctive reality which is to be distinguished both from individuals and relations, although it may include them. It is an object in itself quite apart from its subparts (and it may not even have subparts).

From this analysis, it seems that every unity (whether it be an individual, a relation, or a whole) is as real as any other unity. This means not only that each individual is, from the metaphysical point of view, as real as any other individual, but that any individual is as real as any relation or any whole, including the Whole which encompasses all things (*contra* Tillich). Or, to say it another way, "the Universe" is no more real than any individual within "the Universe" —for the characteristic of reality is unity, and it is as real to be an individual as it is to be a whole. While a whole is "bigger" than certain individuals, it is not ontologically of a higher grade (i. e., not better). Moreover, a whole does not add to or subtract from the reality of the individuals existing "within it." These have their own independent

[9] William James, *Essays in Radical Empiricism* (New York, 1912), p. 42.

G

principle of being (their unity of individuality), and so they are *a se,* and not from the whole. By these arguments, I clearly distinguish my view from those which conclude from the fact that individuals (and/or relations) are in the Whole that they have their being only *from* the Whole. This is not the case. Individuals have their being in the Whole, but *from* themselves; for individuality does not originate in, nor derive from wholeness, nor the reverse. Wholeness, individuality, and relationality are therefore three distinct hypostases of unity. As such, each is capable of being the principle of an independent system of categories. (Moreover, while there are at least these three hypostases of unity, and while I am willing to argue that there are only these three, my analysis permits the possibility that there may be more than these three.)

9. *Unity Is the Principle of Three Distinct Category-Systems*

Because unity (being) is the subject of every predication, we must acknowledge that everything that is said is said *about it.* Therefore, unity is not itself a category-distinction; rather it is the subject of every category-distinction. This means that we can talk about existence only by means of the category-distinctions which are appropriate to it. The classical theological discussion about the proper mode of speaking about the person of Christ (i. e., the unity that constitutes His existence) specifies this point very clearly and formulates the principle as follows: that nothing can be said about the person of Christ immediately, but things can be said about the person of Christ only through the categorical specifications appropriate to that subject.

From the fact that we cannot talk about unity directly, but only by means of the category-distinctions appropriate to it, it follows that unity is the principle of the system of categories. But because there are three quite distinct hypostases of unity, there must also be three quite distinct systems of categories—each of which has one of the hypostases of unity as its principle. These three category-systems are as follows: (1) a category-system which contains the distinctions appropriate to every individual; (2) a category-system which contains the distinctions appropriate to every relation; and (3) a category-system which contains the distinctions appropriate to every whole.

Now it might seem that it cannot be the case that there are three quite independent and self-contained category-systems, since distinctions appropriate to individuals, to relations, and to wholes must appear within a single system if that system is to be complete. For how can a category-system which takes individuality as its principle account for relations at all except by including within itself those categories which are appropriate to relationality, and vice versa? And does this not mean that there are not three independent category-systems, differentiated in accordance with the three notions of unity? For example, is it not the case that the Aristotelian system of categories (which is based on the notion of being as individuality) also accounts for relations? However, this objection is based on a misapprehension. For it fails to see that the three notions of unity are not only the principles of distinct category systems, but also principles implying distinct notions of time, space, causality, truth, and number appropriate to the three systems. These different notions actually make it possible for each of the category-systems to account for phenomena (which we ordinarily think are appropriate to other systems) in terms of themselves alone.

a. For example, Aristotle's view that such seemingly relational distinctions as position, place, and time are merely modifications of individuals can be seen to be correct just as soon as we grant that (from the point of view of individuals per se) space, time, and causality can exist only as qualifications of the state of individuals. According to this understanding, space and time are what we today call "relative." That is, there is no such thing as space or time per se (i. e., empty space or time). Rather, space and time are only categorical modifications of individuals in their interaction. Therefore, on this view, space and time are "plenums" (i. e., all individuals are in full contact with other individuals; their surfaces are fully in contact with other surfaces). Causality, within this understanding of time and space, is by efficiency, or "bumping"—for only individuals are real, and their motion is shifted from one to another by the contact of one with another. Moreover, within this framework of thinking, there is no possibility for such purely formal realities as the square roots of negative numbers; there is no actual infinity, no action at a distance. And even though complex individuals can be abstractly reduced to simpler constituents, it is always the case that these simpler constituents are conceived to belong to the more complex individual, which is differentiated internally in accordance with the distinctions appropriate to the category-system. This more complex individual will then be subsumed under a still more complex individual, and so forth, until we arrive at the all-inclusive and most complex individual, the *finite universe*. From this perspective, it is possible to construct a category-system which is capable of fully explaining all things in terms of the unity of individuality.

b. On the other hand, if we follow our henological analysis to this point, then we must acknowledge that relations have no less claim to be real than do individuals, for they are no less "one" and have no less determinate identity. Since this is the case, there can be a category-system whose subject is relation per se (or "relationship"). This category-system will also depend upon its own appropriate notions of time, space, and causality. Within this system, time and space will be understood as formal, empty, and infinite; moreover, time and space can be conceived to be one dimension, i. e., the space/time dimension. Causality will not be understood as efficiency, but as a harmonious constant conjunction of terms. Given this view of causality and space, all action will be conceived to be at a distance; the world will be an *actual infinite*. Moreover, just as in the system of individuality all relations are understood to be modifications of individuals, so within the system of relationality all individuals will be understood to be nothing other than "relational intersections." Finally, within this general scheme, the system of categories will extend beyond the discriminations appropriate to the Aristotelian system, for it will deal not only with contingently existing individuals, but also with non-existent terms such as possible worlds and negative numbers. This expansion in categorial specifications is possible because the subject of all predication is, in the last analysis, relationality per se ("relationship"). And the relationality of nonexistents and possible-existents is as real as the relationality of existents—for the subject of the relational system of categories (and symbolic logic) is relation considered as an object in its own right.

c. A third possible system of categories may be constructed on the principle of wholeness. Such a system will be capable of encompassing all things within a single scheme of explanation, for it will work with its unique notions of space, time, causality, truth, number, and so forth. Precisely because such a system has not found embodiment in the science of the west, it has never been exhaustively developed (though Goethe proposed exactly such a program of science in his day, and the Gestalt psychologists are developing many of these distinctions in our time). In spite of the fact that a system of categories constructed on the unity of *wholeness* has not yet been scientifically exposed, our analysis shows that it is possible in principle. And, in fact, many of the particular distinctions appropriate to such a system have been specified. So, for example, Boethius noted that there are (at least) two kinds of numbers—the number by which we count and the number inherent in the things counted. "Oneness" (*unitas*) is that by which we count "one thing" (*unum*). So, also, "two" (*duo*) refers to such things as men or stones, but "twoness" (*dualitas*) is that by which men or stones are counted.[10] This distinction between two types of number is further elaborated by Anselm, who notes that the number by which we count is no less a distinct kind of unity than the unity of the thing counted; this number is the unity of *wholeness*. And in his defense of the proposition that we can predicate "three" of something that is one, and "one" of something that is three (in such a way that the three are not predicated of one another), Anselm gives a brilliant illustration of the way in which wholes are numbered:

Suppose there is a spring from which there originates and flows a river, which later accumulates into a lake. And suppose its name is "the Nile." Now we say that the spring, the river, and the lake are different from one another, in such a way that we would not call the spring "the river" or "the lake," nor the river "the spring" or "the lake," nor the lake "the spring" or "the river." And yet the spring is called "the Nile," the river is called "the Nile," and the lake is called "the Nile." Similarly the spring and the river together are called "the Nile," the spring and the lake together are called "the Nile," and the river and the lake together are called "the Nile." And the spring, the river, and the lake, all three together, are called "the Nile." But yet, whether the name "Nile" is applied to them *individually,* or in combinations of two or three, it is always one and the same Nile—there is not one Nile in this place and another Nile in that. The spring, the river, and the lake, therefore, are three, and are at the same time one Nile, one stream, one nature, one water. And none of these things can be said to be three. For there are neither three Niles, streams, natures, or waters, nor three springs, rivers, or lakes. Here is an example, therefore, in which "one" is predicated of what is three, and "three" of what is one, and yet the three are not predicated of one another.

Now if my opponent objects that neither the spring, the river, nor the lake singularly, nor any two of them, is the complete Nile, but only part of it, let him consider this. The *whole* Nile, from where it begins to where

10 Boethius, *De Trinitate,* 3.

it comes to an end, exists, as it were, through its *whole* "lifetime." It never exists wholly and simultaneously in any time or place, but exists through its parts, and it will not be complete until it ceases to exist. For in this respect it is somewhat like a prayer, which, as long as it is "pouring forth," as it were, from the "spring" of the mouth, is not complete; when it is complete, it has already come to an end. Now if anyone were to examine the matter in this way, and to understand it carefully, he would realise that the *whole* Nile is the spring, the *whole* Nile is the river, and the *whole* Nile is the lake, and that the spring is not the river or the lake, the river is not the lake or the spring, and the lake is not the spring or the river. For the spring is not the same as the river or the lake, even though the river and the lake are what the spring is, i. e., the same Nile, the same stream, the same water, the same nature. This is a case, therefore, in which "three" is predicated of one complete *whole,* and "one complete *whole"* is predicated of three, and yet the three are not predicated of one another.[11]

From this example, we note that the mode of time and space appropriate to "wholes" is omnipresence; i. e., the whole is archetypally and fully present in all its parts. Hence, we say of "the universe" that it is fully present in every "flower in the crannied wall," just as we say of a nation (e. g. "America") that it is fully present in every rock and rill, in its every part. It is for this reason that the time and space of wholeness may be called archetypal, for every part of a whole may be regarded not only as what it is in itself, but also as a presentation of the whole to which it belongs. Hence, after Jesus Christ has ascended into heaven so that he fills all things (i. e., becomes their whole), he is the archetype of the world and is ·really present in any and every part of it.

Just as the mode of time and space appropriate to wholes is "omnipresence," so the mode of causality is "participation." And from this also follows a definition of truth as a felt "rightness" (Anselm) or "requiredness" (the Gestalt psychologists). In our day, the major contributions to understanding the categorical specifications appropriate to wholes are being made by psychologists (Köhler, Max Wertheimer), phenomenologists of religion (Eliade, Frankfort, Jacobsen), and literary critics (Robbe-Grillet, Frye). In the previous essay on myth, I have considered other aspects of this hypostasis of unity.

[11] Anselm of Canterbury, *Epistola de Incarnatione Verbi,* ch. 13; G. Peck, trans., in *Anselm of Canterbury, Theological Treatises,* Vol. II, J. Hopkins and H. Richardson, eds. (Cambridge, Mass., 1966), pp. 99-101. (My italics.)

10. *The Problem of a Plurality of Category-Systems*

The legitimacy of three independent systems of categories, each based on its own distinct notion of unity, raises a fundamental problem. For since every theory of meaning and explanation presupposes a determinate notion of unity, then we know that any of the three kinds of unity can become the principle of an entire philosophic world view —a world view which can not only claim to explain all reality in a systematic and exhaustive manner, but can also make good on this claim. Each of these philosophic world views can make good on its claim because it is able, on the basis of its categorical specifications, to give a scientific determination to all things (e. g., Aristotle's explanation of relations as aspects of individuals, or Edwards's account of individuals as relational intersections).

Moreover, because every philosophy based on one of the three possible systems of categories can give an exhaustive account of reality consistent with its determinate criteria of meaning and truth, it also may propose a prescriptive theory of linguistic meaning. Through this theory, it then counts statements which are consistent with its category-system as meaningful and counts all other statements as meaningless. Paul Weiss describes this problem as follows:

Opposition is a symmetrical relation. It requires that there be two sides, each denying, rejecting, negating the other. Let us term two sides A and B, and let us term the languages which do justice to the structure, meaning, divisions of A and B, languages *a* and *b*. As complete and independent, *a* and *b* are logically distinct, coordinate languages; each makes distinctions the other does not acknowledge. From the standpoint of of language *a*, language *b* is said to speak *meaninglessly* so far as it makes distinctions which *a* does not permit, and is said to speak *confusedly* so far as it does not make distinctions which *a* makes or requires. From the standpoint of language *b*, similar observations are to be made regarding language *a*. In summary, this is the structure of all polemics.[12]

My analysis of the intrinsic necessity of a multiplicity of category-systems not only accounts for the situation Weiss describes, but also suggests a way to overcome it. For there is no way to avoid this problem, nor can we deny the legitimacy of that intellectual attitude which systematically hones all understanding to the precise discriminations appropriate to the various notions of unity, and attempts to de-

[12] Paul Weiss, *Modes of Being* (Carbondale, Ill., 1958), p. 366 f.

velop specialized languages. Moreover, we must even acknowledge that because each category-system is based on a determinate notion of unity (existence), all three systems make an equal claim upon us. My analysis reveals, therefore, an intrinsic demand for a theory of polysemous (or manifold) explanation. And the problem we must face is how we can maintain such a theory of meaning without giving way to utter skepticism or relativism. For does not the very manifold-ness of the category-systems require us to acknowledge that reality is not one, but many? And does not the fact that no one category-system is intrinsically superior to any other lead us into relativism? As Northrop Frye remarks: "Once we have admitted the principle of polysemous meaning, we can either stop with a purely relative and pluralistic position or we can go on to consider the possibility that there is a finite number of valid critical methods, and that they can all be contained in a single theory."[13]

The whole intent of my analysis thus far is to show that, in fact, the plurality of critical methods can be contained in a single finite theory. For, as we have seen, the very *plurality* of critical methods (i. e., methods dependent upon precise category-systems and methods of unitizing and explaining) grows out of the fact that unity itself is a complex term which implies a certain kind of plurality. Hence, my argument that we must use all the possible category-systems has a certain logical principle behind it, namely, that each is an hypostasis of oneness. By noting this logical necessity of employing all the possible category-systems, I distinguish my argument from that of the relativists, who recognize the legitimacy of using all available category-systems (or models, or root metaphors) but deny that there is any necessary reason for our employing all these systems (e. g., Pepper and Dilthey). Moreover, my position is distinguished from the rela-tivists in that I recognize that all the different category-systems are ultimately one and not many. For the relativist speaks of the many kinds of explanation as being many; but I speak of them as being one. But how can we understand them to be one, i. e., how can we understand there to be "a finite number of critical methods which can all be contained in a single theory"? I shall now give an argument to show how we may do so, and why one must require every full explanation to utilize those forms and meanings appropriate to (at least) the three distinct category-systems I have outlined. Thereby

[13] Northrop Frye, *Anatomy of Criticism* (New York, 1966), p. 72.

we shall see the justification for the insight that governs the meta-disciplines: that all meaning and explanation is polysemous in principle.

LANGUAGE LEVELS AND POLYSEMOUS EXPLANATIONS

11. *The Types of Explanation*

We have seen that there is an intrinsic connection between a theory of explanation (category-systems, meaning, even language) and a theory of reality. My contention that being is unity implies a poly-semous theory of explanation in accordance with the multiplicity of hypostases of unity. The various ontologies that have been proposed in the history of thought have also implied distinctive explanatory procedures. A useful method for approaching our argument that the three category-systems are also one with one another will be to sum-marize the various possible theories of explanation, indicating when each has been used in the past.

a. Monothematic Explanations. These explanations operate wholly within a single category-system and utilize a single criterion of mean-ing and truth. For example, Mill and Strawson seek to explain things empirically, unitizing reality by means of the category-system appro-priate to individuality. Monothematic explanations are characteristic of the modern period (*circa* 1600-1900) and are the reason for the great critical power of the special sciences, which determine, integrate, and judge all things on the same level and in terms of a single system of categories.

b. Bi- and Trithematic Explanations. Someone may prefer to ex-plain all things within a single category-system, but may also acknowl-edge that one category-system is not sufficient to encompass all things. He may propose, therefore, that reality comes in one or more types, and that one explanation procedure is appropriate to dealing with one type of reality while another procedure is appropriate for dealing with another. This will lead to bithematic explanations. Bi-thematic explanations are found especially in the late modern period (*circa* 1850-1950) and represent an attempt to maintain the modern monothematic principle by proposing that it be multiplied so that two category-systems will be applied to two different kinds of objects. For example, the late nineteenth-century distinction between *Natur-*

wissenschaften and *Geisteswissenschaften* falls into this class. Or again, W. Stace utilizes the bithematic pattern when he proposes that there are two different, though equally critical, methods for understanding two types of reality: "Time" and "Eternity." In the same way, the number of terms and explanation procedures can be multiplied to three (trithematic) or more (polythematic). Those who contend that there are a multiplicity of objects of human interest, each of which involves its own *independent* language, assert that explanation is polythematic.

Note that the movement from monothematic explanations to bi- and trithematic explanations still utilizes the principle of monothematic explanations. For every reality is held to be wholly encompassable within a single category-system. But the number of category-systems is multiplied in accordance with the multiplication of different kinds of objects, and it is not held that two or more category-systems are appropriate to the *same object*.

c. *Seriothematic Explanations*. Now it may be proposed that there are a multiplicity of category-systems, and that these systems may be applied to the same object, but not at the same time. Hence, they are applied *serially*. The justification for this assertion may be the claim either that (1) reality itself processes through a number of metaphysical stages, to each of which a different intellectual mode is appropriate, or that (2) human knowledge of reality has processed through a number of historical stages, to each of which a different intellectual mode is appropriate. A representative of the first position is Hegel. A representative of the second is Comte, who holds that reality has been successively understood by means of the religious, metaphysical, and scientific modes. In seriothematic explanations there is the systematic thoroughness characteristic of monothematic explanations (for the object is never considered under more than one category-system at any given time). However, there is a greater richness than in monothematic explanations, since the object is considered serially under two or more category-systems. Seriothematic explanations have especially flourished in conjunction with process philosophies, and they possess a certain prima-facie appeal. But, as I have shown, they are all ultimately based on the fundamental error of those metaphysics which confuse being itself with a certain kind of being (in this case "process").

d. *Cross-thematic Explanations*. This type of explanation is characteristic of classical philosophy and is still defended by certain contemporary thinkers. Classical thinkers tend to oppose a rigorous critical distinction of a plural number of category-systems, and propose a direct approach to experience which bypasses a prior concern with epistemological and methodological questions. I suggest that a proper term to describe the classical explanation procedure is cross-thematic, for it proceeds on the assumption that questions appropriate to one realm of life can be also asked of other realms; that, for example, the principle of causality can be applied to metaphysical entities if it is also applied to empirical entities (e. g., Sillem's strong argument).[14] Such an explanation procedure "crosses" or "mixes" the realms, and thus fails to attain full conceptual clarity. In Weiss's terms, it speaks "confusedly."

Cross-thematic explanations do take greater account of the richness of things in any given moment, but they do so by losing the critical force and clarity that characterize modern monothematic explanations. The failure to attain full conceptual clarity is then imputed to the object of knowledge (or the degree of adequation between the object and the mind) rather than to the failure to develop a critical epistemology. This can be evidenced by the fact that the following Aristotelian dictum is repeated again and again in the later classical tradition: "It is the mark of an educated man to look for precision in each class of things just so far as the nature of the subject admits."[15] But such a formula can hardly be cited today as an excuse for not undertaking a critical epistemological and methodological inquiry prior to the study of any particular object. Hence, the classical explanation procedure can no longer be vindicated as a sufficiently rigorous method of understanding.

e. Triune-thematic Explanations (polysemous). Now the only remaining alternative, and the one I shall defend, is that the only adequate explanation is one that speaks of the same object as if it were three different hypostases and therefore uses all three category-systems simultaneously, without however "crossing" or "mixing" the three. I shall vindicate this claim by showing that this threefold explanation

[14] Edward Sillem, *Ways of Thinking about God* (London, 1961), ch. 7.

[15] Aristotle, *Nichomachean Ethics,* I, 3, W. D. Ross, trans., in *The Basic Works of Aristotle,* R. McKeon, ed. (New York, 1941), p. 936. For its continued use in the tradition of classical philosophy see Thomas Aquinas, *Summa contra Gentiles,* I, 3; and fn. 4 to this text in the Marietti edition (Rome, 1961), p. 4.

is the only explanation of things as *one.* For this reason I call it triune-thematic. Such an explanation is neither single (monothematic), serial, nor mixed (cross-thematic); rather, it is polysemous. It is characteristic of such explanations to employ the device of "triplication of categories" in order to account for the object in its triune oneness, or being. And, as we have seen, polysemous explanations in accordance with some (explicit or assumed) theory of unity are characteristic of the contemporary metacritical disciplines, and the shift toward this type of explanation is the decisive evidence that the "modern period" of western history has come to an end and that we are now entering a new historical epoch.

We find anticipations of the polysemous theory of explanation in certain Christian theologians of the past, many of whom even used the device of the triplication of categories. For example, the Lutheran theologian Quenstedt speaks of man under "three essences": Man is "able not to die" in relation to his creaturehood; he is "not able not to die" in relation to his fallenness; and he is "not able to die" in relation to his redemption.[16] Now, when we recall the Lutheran description of these three states as *simul,* then we have a clear example of the "triplication of categories." (Of course Augustine's discrimination of three abilities of free choice with respect to sin is the device Quenstedt is utilizing, but Augustine tends to treat these abilities serially; so in his hands the formula is seriothematic.) It is common today to suggest that theological statements such as Quenstedt's are "paradoxical" (and hence nonrational or even irrational). But such a suggestion comes from those who are committed to the principle of monothematic explanation; for these typical theological explanations are neither paradoxical nor even mixed, but are polysemous explanations which more or less consciously employ the device of the triplication of categories.

Elsewhere I have suggested why polysemous explanations intrinsically characterize the method of Christian theology.[17] But we find anticipations of this explanation procedure also arising from non-theological concerns. For example, the poet Coleridge, in his theory of language, writes that someone "may convey truth in any one of three possible languages—that of the Sense, as objects appear to the beholder on this earth; or that of Science, which supposes the

[16] J. A. Quenstedt, *Theologia Didactico-Polemica,* II, 7; cited from Heinrich Schmid, *Doctrinal Theology of the Evangelical Lutheran Church* (Minneapolis, 1899), p. 228.
[17] Secularism and Faith, *The Current* 6[3-4] (1966), 26-30.

beholder placed in the center; or that of Philosophy, which resolves both into a supersensual reality."[18]

From Coleridge's suggestion that there are "three possible languages," we can begin to move toward understanding the unity of the many realms of meaning, i. e., their *triunity*. For it is not strictly possible to have three languages, as Coleridge contends. But there is a certain complexity in language which accords with what he intends. By analyzing this complexity, we can move toward understanding the unity of the three kinds of unity.

12. *Language: Three Levels of Meaning*

Language is a complex phenomenon which involves three distinct modes of meaning, consistent with the three category-systems I have discussed. It should be noted, however, that we do not have three languages; we have only one language, which, considered in its complex unity, we call "ordinary language." Like reality itself, we encounter ordinary language as a rich unity, and we cannot separate the three hypostases of reality within it, for these three realms run together. But, within this ordinary language we can distinguish three different levels of meaning—i. e., language has the meanings appropriate to individuals, relations, and wholes. Yet, though we may try to distinguish these levels of meaning by constructing three separate languages (a language descriptive of individuals, a language of relations, and a language of wholes), we can never fully accomplish this end. For these three "languages" are only abstractions, or ideals, in terms of which we analyze the rich complexity of our ordinary language. This ordinary unity of language is an external manifestation of the intrinsic unity of the three realms.

We can distinguish these three levels of language by considering how we would answer the question of a person who asks, "What do you mean when you say that?"

a. Now someone may not understand what we mean because he does not understand the signification of a word we are using. For example, if I say, "There is a Tutterstrudel in my office and I am afraid to go home today because of it," you will not know what I mean because you do not know what a Tutterstrudel is. In this case, the meaning of my sentence can be made clear by explaining, or

[18] Samuel Taylor Coleridge, *Confessions of an Inquiring Spirit,* H. Hart, ed. (Stanford, Calif., 1957), p. 43.

pointing out, or enacting the thing which the word signifies. The process by which we do this is a subject of some discussion: some argue that we must be able to produce a sense impression; others argue that it is sufficient to make clear its relation, or resemblance, to something that is already known. This way of dealing with a misunderstanding presupposes the notion of language as a reference system, wherein words are signs of facts, and where the criterion of truth is correspondence.

b. But it may be that someone's failure to understand what I mean is not on this level. For example, consider Augustine's suggestion that "The present is no time at all."[19] Someone might understand the meaning of each word in this sentence (just as he might understand each word in the sentence "God is three in one"), but might not understand the meaning of the assertion that "the present is no time." In this case, what is confusing him is not the signification of the individual signs, but their use in these determinate relations. He might say that he does not understand how the "present" can be no "time," since we experience the present and we divide "time" into "past, present, and future." Augustine would reply that what this person fails to understand is the proper relations, or unitions, which these distinctive words have with one another. For words not only signify determinate objects, but they also have certain relations to one another by which they can be combined into meaningful sentences. In order to solve the question of meaning when all the terms appear to be understood individually, but their connections in a single sentence seem unclear, we must explicate the relations proper to the terms themselves. Hence, Augustine explains his assertion by showing that the meaning of the word "present" may finally be determined not referentially but relationally—by showing how it operates between "past" and "future." In this relation, "present" means no time, but a point (or nontemporal moment) which divides the duration of the past from the duration of the future. The meaning of Augustine's assertion is, therefore, understood by grasping the mutual *relation* of the terms at stake.

In case (a), then, the meaning of words is determined by their reference to a world of individuals; in case (b), by their being ordered in a realm of relations. The linguistic unit proper to the realm of

[19] Augustine, *Confessions,* XI, esp. 14-30. (The sentence under discussion is not found *verbatim* in the *Confessions,* but is composed by the present writer in accordance with the third level of meaning in language.)

individuals is the word; the linguistic unit proper to the realm of relations is the sentence.

c. Now, it may be the case that a person has understood each individual word I have uttered, and has understood the relation of all the words in each of the sentences I have uttered, but still has not understood what I intend. For example: in the College Board tests, the student is required to read a paragraph and then answer the question "Which of the following phrases best summarizes the point of this paragraph?" This implies that the given paragraph intends to express some point, some central idea; but, the idea cannot be given expression except through the paragraph itself. Rather, it can be presented as a sensible or linguistic object only through a story. It is a whole, or a unity which exceeds all its parts, though it comes to expression through them. The unity of the whole, or the Gestalt that unites all its parts, is symbolized in its image, or title.

Most failures to get at the meaning of theological and philosophical discourse are of this third type. That is, even after we know the meaning of the individual words and individual sentences, we still fail to grasp the general idea they are trying to express through their "paragraphal" and "discoursal" unity. This is not surprising, for the ability to grasp the single idea which a discourse is trying to express is the highest, and most difficult, act of the mind. It is common today for many persons who are unable to grasp meaning on this level of wholeness to deny even that there is any such meaning. However, the fact remains that this ability to grasp the idea of a discourse can be developed through disciplined training and experience, and the question whether a given discourse is meaningful is, in the last analysis, for persons trained in the particular discourse to decide.

13. *The Complex Unity of Ordinary Language*

Because the three levels of meaning in language are related to three distinct kinds of unity and category-systems, it is always possible to propose, as an ideal, that we separate three distinct languages out from the complex unity of ordinary language, and that we work with these three languages individually. So, for example, a given scientific discipline may, for the sake of special clarity, attempt to construct and work with a purely referential language; or a poet may attempt to work with a wholly nonreferential language, depending simply on metaphors and unique conjunctions of words and images in order to evoke a feeling of some whole—to give a "total experience." Such specialized languages can be approximated through disciplined abstraction and rigorous control. However, we should remember that these approximations to specialized languages are abstractions from the rich unity of ordinary language, where the many levels of meaning flow together; and we should not be surprised to discover that any specialized language, however carefully constructed, will contain remnants of meaning from the other realms. Moreover, since we recognize that these approximations to specialized languages are abstractions created from primary speech, we do not have any problem of finding a way to unite them. There would be a problem of uniting them if they were, in fact, three primary languages; but they are not. They are, rather, abstractions from primary language, and this primary language is itself a concrete complex unity.

We can call this ordinary language *precritical,* and the specialized languages *critical.* Ordinary language is precritical because the different levels of meaning flow together and blur ("cross-thematic explanations"); specialized languages are critical because they utilize systematic categorical distinctions (mono-, bi-, and trithematic explanations). The reason that ordinary language and experience tends to grasp things in their (precritical) unity is because the three realms of reality are one, and hence tend to run together or "perichorese." This tendency of the three realms of meaning to perichorese in ordinary experience is, in fact, a sign that the three realms are all one and that they are within one another. Moreover, this tendency of language and experience to perichorese is the main obstacle to the attempt to construct "pure languages" which confine themselves to a single realm of meaning and expression. Because of this tendency, referential language will always be infused with mythic tendencies, and vice versa.

We must now move on to consider the henological unity of the three realms themselves, and not rest satisfied with the mere evidence of a tendency toward their unity in ordinary language and experience.

THE UNITY OF THE UNITIES

14. *That There Is a Unity of the Three Unities*

We have seen that unity is a term which is capable of designating what it means "to be," and that unity is distinguished into three hypostases, each of which may be the principle of a category-system which determines a certain type of meaning. We have seen that such a theory accounts for the polysemous explanations that characterize contemporary meta-disciplines. But we have not yet either presented an argument for the unity of the three realms or suggested what the character of this unity might be.

The following discussion of these questions might also be construed as a suggestion toward a henological argument determining the existence and nature of God. In fact, my proposal resembles Peirce's "Neglected Argument" for the reality of God, who is "really creator of all three Universes of Experience."[20] It begins with the assumption of critical epistemology that there is a plural number of explanation procedures, or category-systems, and then argues for their ultimate metaphysical unity. Peirce called the ultimate metaphysical unity of two such realms of meaning "the reality of thirdness." But I call it "the unity of the unities" (for I am committed only to the principle that there are at least three realms, and I have presented no argument in this essay to show that three is necessarily a complete number). Moreover, my argument will differ from Peirce's in that it presents logical as well as empirical considerations in behalf of the contention that the many realms of experience are ultimately unified. Peirce argued that the fact of the progress of the theoretical and applied sciences is an evidence that there exists a "Thirdness" which unites "Firstness" and "Secondness"—these three realms roughly expressing the distinct objects of "the triad: feeling, volition, cognition."[21] I have suggested that a similar argument might be made from the unity of the various levels of meaning in ordinary language. But I also wish to note that a henological analysis of the plurality of realms of

[20] Charles Peirce, *Collected Papers,* C. Hartshorne and P. Weiss, eds. (Cambridge, Mass., 1960), VI, par. 452, p. 311.

[21] *Ibid.,* I, par. 322, p. 166. Although it is fashionable today to disparage faculty psychology as a vestige of medieval thought, we should note that Peirce held a somewhat analogous position. "The triad, feeling, volition, cognition, is usually regarded as a purely psychological division. Long series of experiments, persistent and much varied, though only qualitative, have left me little doubt, if any, that there are in those elements three quite disparate modes of awareness. That is a psychological proposition; but that which now concerns us is not psychological, particularly; namely the differences between *that of which we are aware* in feeling, volition, and cognition [my italics]." My position is similar to Peirce's, although I distinguish the three modes of awareness as different ways in which the self is one. This allows us to acknowledge that "feeling, volition, and cognition" (psychologically considered) can all be present in each of the modes of awareness—though in different orders.

H

meaning also allows us to bring forth certain logical considerations for their unity, and will lead us to a different understanding of the character of this unity than that held by Peirce.

Suppose, then, that someone were to argue that there is no unity of the realms that have been discriminated above. This argument might be sustained if it could be shown that each of the three realms is *sui generis*. There would be, in consequence, three disunified possible explanation systems, any one, two, or three of which might be employed. On this view, there is no necessity for regarding the three realms as one. This argument, however, has forgotten that individuality, relationality, and wholeness are three types of *unity;* i. e., it has slipped into regarding them as three distinct essences, or kinds of being, and (looking at them from the point of view of ontology) sees neither a way to regard them as one nor a way to regard a conflict among them as meaningful. However, such a conclusion is false because each of the realms is governed by a principle of unity, and therefore it is meaningful to ask about their unity with one another.

Let us acknowledge that the discussion of the unity of the three unities presents us with a unique difficulty. For language is inappropriate to describe *this* unity. This is the case because language presupposes a system of categories and always speaks about a unity which is the principle of that system. But the unity of the unities is not the immediate subject of any single category-system, and hence cannot be spoken of. So our language will always be inadequate for discussing this problem. For we can only ask about the unity of the three by using language that suggests that the unity of the three is one of the three. So, for example, if we ask how they are *all* one, we are suggesting that the unity of the three is the unity of wholeness; or, if we ask how the three are *related,* we do the same thing with respect to relationality; or if we ask how they are *each* one, then we are suggesting that the unity of unities is an individual.

This intrinsic limitation of our language does not mean that we can say nothing at all, however. For we can approximately determine the unity of these three by (1) understanding why we cannot express the unity of these three unities except by a regulative notion which cannot be the subject of direct predication, even though it controls and guides our thinking on all levels (the principle of the sovereignty of God over thought). And (2) we can come to this understanding by eliminating the improper ways of explaining the unity of unties.

15. *How the Three Unities Are One*

a. The unity of the three is not one of the three. The unity of the three cannot be one of the three because all three have equal claim to ultimacy. That is, no one of the three could claim to be the "genus" of all the three, because it is just as much a member of the fundamental henological class as either of the other two. This fact may not be easily understood, for we have just seen that language always suggests that the unity of the realms is one (of the three types). And this is precisely why nonhenological ontologies have a certain apparent viability. But we should argue the contrary: the fact that we can speak about the unity of the unities in each of three linguistic ways shows that no one of these three determinations has any special claim to be the unity of the three unities.

There is no way out of the linguistic problem. But this fact, far from being an objection to my theory, is a confirmation of it—for I have already argued that the unity of the unities cannot be the proper object of language because it is not the subject of any single category-system; i. e., it is a transcategorical reality.

b. The unity of the three is not a fourth hypostasis of unity which utterly transcends the three and always remains unknown. Even if we do not claim to know what the distinctive hypostatic differentiation of this fourth unity is (or if we claim it is totally undifferentiated), we still find the following objection to such a notion: the unity of the three cannot be a fourth, for then we would have to know what the unity of the fourth with the three was, and this would lead to an infinite regress. Therefore, it is not only incorrect, but also useless, to invoke a fourth unity as the unity of the three.

c. The unity of the three is not absolute nothing. If we were to affirm that the unity of the three is absolute nothing, then (1) we would be saying that that which is common to all being is nothing. But this is a contradiction, for it is equivalent to asserting that what is common to all ones is null. (2) We would also be saying that there is nothing rather than something. But the presupposition of our whole analysis is that there is something, and we cannot deny the presupposition of our analysis once the analysis has finally come to its conclusion simply because we do not like the conclusion. If a person wants to assert that the final term is nothing, then he may certainly do so; but he may not do so at this point in the argument. For he has already granted that there is something by proceeding this far.

d. The unity of the three is not relative nothing, i. e., the negation of some determinate being. For example, when we say, "There is nothing there," we mean to reject the assertion that "there is something there." In this case, the nothing asserted is not absolute nothing, but relative nothing (for it signifies the negation of a real or possible something). Now, it is true that the unity of the three is a relative nothing, i. e., not a whole, not an individual, and not a relation. For the unity of the three is not one of the three. But although we agree that this answer is correct, it has not yet determined our understanding of this unity.

e. The unity of the three is the three themselves. I have reduced our alternatives to this final one, and, as we shall see, there are no objections to it except for the fact that it is novel. That is, oneness is nothing other than the threeness of these three ones. This is what oneness is, for we see that each is one, and oneness is fully in each, and yet oneness is fully in all. This accounts for the fact that each one can be the principle of a category-system which is perfectly exhaustive; and it accounts for the fact that there are three category-systems; and it accounts for the fact that we must regard all three category-systems as one.

From another point of view, it accounts for the fact that unity is not something that transcends all things, but is present in all things. That is, unity is the principle of absolute universality, and in fact drives towards a multiplication (triplication) of itself. It exists in three existences, or hypostases, each of which is a distinctive unity. Moreover, because each of the three is fully unity, the One itself is fully present in each and is fully present in all.[22]

Because the unity of the three is nothing other than the three themselves, and because whatever is in all three is also in each one, we may also say that all things (and not only unity) exist in three independent hypostases. Moreover, however unusual this assertion may sound when formulated in this direct way, it is nothing other than a summary of the way in which we ordinarily think and speak of all things anyway. For we think of a piece of steel as being an individual,

---

[22] This solution for the problem of the unity of the unities will hold true even if there are more than three hypostases of unity. For if there are four hypostases, then the unity of the unities will be "the four themselves"; if five, then "the five themselves"; etc. This is why the argument of this essay is independent of the question of the number of kinds of unity that must ultimately be accounted for.

and yet we think of it as being contained absolutely within the relational system which embraces all reality. Note that the candid assertion that this piece of steel exists in these two hypostases solves the metaphysical quandary which arises when we think of the steel as only an individual thing and then ask how we can understand it mathematically (i. e., relationally). The same kind of double existence of *persons* is also presupposed by cybernetic systems.

In religious statements, the principle of the threefold existence of things is assumed and is the basis of many typical statements (e. g., Quenstedt's statement, discussed above). So Paul writes that he lives, yet not be, but Christ; that he prays, yet in him also the Spirit. Or again, it is said both that "God is All and man is nothing," and that "God is one being and man is another." Or again, we do things both freely and by God's will. Or again, the cross of Christ is an individual event within the whole of reality, and yet it is Reality Itself. Now these typical religious statements can best be explained not by invoking the category of paradox, but by assuming the triplicated existence of all things to which this complex mode of speaking (the triplication of categories and assertions) is appropriate. For from the fact that the unity of the three unities is nothing other than the three themselves, we see not only the legitimacy, but even the necessity, of such polysemous ways of speaking.

THE HENOLOGICAL ARGUMENT FOR GOD

16. *The Transcendent Unity of the Unities is God*

The arguments presented in sections 14 and 15 of this chapter complete the outline of a henological metaphysics. My conclusion has neither qualified the three realms of unity by making them modes of something else (Thomas), nor denied the ultimacy of each of these three realms by adverting to "the One" which transcends them (Plotinus). Rather, since the unity of the unities is the three themselves, we may say that every unity is a being, and that the realm of thought and experience is coincident with the realm of being. Yet, to account for these consistent henological assertions, we must affirm not only the reality of each of the three unities (individuality, relationality, and wholeness), but also the reality of "the unity of the unities." For the reasons I have given above, this "unity of the unities" cannot be thought or expressed, since it is not the true subject of any single category-system or any level of language. Yet my analysis shows how we should conceive this unity to transcend (or exceed) thought and language even while it establishes their possibility.[23]

My discussion of the unity of the unities may be construed as a suggestion for a henological argument determining the nature and existence of God. This is the case for two reasons.

1. The argument is a metaphysical demonstration of the necessary existence of a being who must be conceived not only to transcend all other beings, but also to determine the manner of their existence. It is common in the philosophical tradition of the west to name a being with such defining characteristics as "God," and to call demonstrations of the existence of this being "proofs for the existence of God." It should be noted that my argument not only purports to determine the necessary existence of such a transcendent being (He is a being, because He is one), but it does so within a general metaphysical position which attempts to vindicate the meaningfulness of such terms as "transcendence" and "necessary being." Thereby it attempts to overcome a priori objections to the legitimacy of these concepts.

2. It may be argued, of course, that my proposal does not result in proving the existence of "God," but only the existence of "the Transcendent One" who is the unity of the unities. For the metaphysics which has been developed takes "the One" (and not "God") as the principle of ultimate reality. And unless it introduces a definition of God as "the One," the argument does not demonstrate the existence of God. However, I do wish to propose just such a definition, on the basis of the biblical experience of the meaning of the name "God." "Hear, O Israel, the Lord our God, the Lord is One" [or "unique"] (Deut. 6:4). In this formula "God" names the unique transcendent One of biblical experience; in this essay, I have tried to show how it is possible to conceive of such a transcendent One. Hence, my essay may be regarded as a henological affirmation of the existence of the God of Israel and the Church.

These biblical considerations are, of course, not intended as philosophical arguments. For by linking the name "God" to the transcendent

[23] In this essay I am proposing a special determination of the concept of transcendence, namely that this concept is meaningful even though we cannot express it through a model or an analogy. In place of a "model" of divine transcendence, I am suggesting that the meaning of this concept is specified in conjunction with (and as the *terminus* of) a method. Hence, the concept of God is inseparable from the (natural and universal) method by which He is attained.

One whom we have attained through metaphysical analysis, we are invoking the authority of a positive religious tradition. The argument by which we connect the biblical name "God" with "the Transcendent One" is theological. But the reason for introducing such an argument at this point is that it allows us to see how a philosophical henology is open to theological use (even though it does not require completion by theology). For the definition "God = the Transcendent One" establishes an identity between the first principles of theology ("God") and philosophy ("the One"); this identity is the basis of a continuity between these two desciplines which must be maintained if theological statements are to be truth claims. (We might recall that Tillich attempted to establish just such a principle of continuity when he asserted—but later repudiated— that the sole nonsymbolic theological statement is that "God is Being Itself."[24]) Only if there is such a principle of continuity between philosophical propositions and the affirmations of faith can the latter be understood to be true, i. e., talking about what is really the case.

17. Toward a Christian Philosophy

Even though the henological metaphysics which I am proposing is open to theology, it should clearly be understood that it is not a theological (or fideistic) metaphysics. For the theory is developed by rational analysis and in terms of natural criteria. It does not invoke revelation at any point, nor does it inquire into the mysteries of faith. (I wish especially to emphasize that "the unity of the unities" is not intended to be an explanation of the Divine Trinity—however useful a trinitarian analogy it may be.) I have found certain Christian formulations to be philosophically suggestive. But there is a difference between the origin of ideas and their validation; and it is with respect to the issue of validation (and the concomitant claim that certain

[24] Tillich's revised position can be seen in the contrast between the following two statements: "The statement that God is being-itself is a nonsymbolic statement. It does not point beyond itself. It means what it says directly and properly. . . ." Paul Tillich, *Systematic Theology, Vol. I* (Chicago, 1951), p. 238, and, "Thus it follows that everything religion has to say about God, including his qualities, actions, and manifestations, has a symbolic character and that the meaning of 'God' is completely missed if one takes the symbolic language literally. But, after this has been stated, the question arises (and has risen in public discussion) as to whether there is a point at which a non-symbolic assertion about God must be made. There is such a point, namely, the statement that everything we say about God is symbolic." *Systematic Theology, Vol. II* (Chicago, 1957), p. 9.

things are universally the case) that I understand my proposal in this essay to be philosophical. Given the availability of the henological system for theological use, and given the fact that many of its fundamental insights have been suggested by Christian faith, I am not averse to calling henology a "Christian philosophy." But even a Christian philosophy must be philosophy, i. e., it must satisfy the criteria proposed by every rational man, whatever his belief or unbelief.

The definition of Christian philosophy which I have proposed is minimal. Hence, it allows a number of philosophical options to claim this name. But even these vary from one another with respect to their facilitating or impelling the understanding and communication of particular theological insights. Of these various options, henology especially facilitates the elaboration of a theology for a sociotechnic age. It presupposes a nonideological metacritical standpoint which seeks not to exclude, but to reconcile, conflicting philosophical commitments. For henology does not affirm yet another conception of being alongside existing ontological options. Rather, it attempts to affirm that which is necessary to every ontology, namely, that whatever being is said to be, it must be said to be one. By insisting upon the unity of all possible ontologies, henology is in a position to reconcile and make material use of all their fundamental affirmations. Thus henology can thereby both explain the legitimate claims of modern relativism and yet show the way beyond this cul-de-sac.

Another advantage of henology over alternative metaphysical options is its adequacy for articulating the implications of a theology which understands the essence of Christianity to be the revelation of the mystery of Divine Unity (i. e., Trinity). To be sure, such an understanding of the essence of Christianity has not been dominant in the western tradition—which has defined God not primarily as Trinity, but as The Good, or Truth, or Being Itself, or Agape, or The Wholly Other, and so forth. However, in the Orthodox tradition (and to some extent in both Calvinism and modern Roman Catholicism), the Trinity is affirmed to be "the basic truth of the Christian faith."[25] I agree with this judgment and with its intention, namely, that all other aspects of revelation originate in and express the Trinity. A theology which un-

[25] For the difference between eastern and western conceptions of the essence of Christianity, see the discussion of The Basis of the World Council of Churches in *The New Delhi Report* (New York, 1962), 152-59. The Orthodox defended the trinitarian addition to the WCC basis as ". . . no attempt at confessionalism, but a short and scriptural statement of the basic truth of the Christian faith."

derstands Christianity to be essentially a revelation of the mystery of Divine Triunity, however, needs to be developed in continuity with a philosophical henology so that there will be continuity between its dogmatic definitions and the forms of natural understanding. In a future volume, I hope to develop this trinitarian interpretation of Christianity and show how it is illuminated by being presented in conjunction with the materials I have developed here.

In the previous four essays we have considered historical and philosophical questions. The next essay, however, deals with questions relating to Christian doctrine. Doctrinal theology is concerned to state the content of revelation in systematic propositional form. While all theology is not doctrinal theology, doctrinal theology is a necessary accompaniment of revelation. For if anything, however limited, is claimed to be revelation, some attempt must be made to state its content. Modern Christianity tends to resist the enterprise of doctrinal theology; but it is the intellectual work of a responsible Church. For even the simplest religious affirmation (e. g., "Jesus is Lord") has presuppositions and implications. A man, even a Christian man, should not affirm one thing and deny the things it presupposes and implies. Doctrinal theology explores these presuppositions and implications.

Previously I have argued that the recent emergence of metacritical consciousness suggests new methods for investigating intellectual problems and displaying our knowledge. In the next essay, I shall attempt this new approach to Christian doctrine by raising three heuristic "meta-questions": *cur creatio, cur deus homo,* and *cur spiritus sanctus*? (Why did God create the world, why did He become man, and why does He send the Holy Spirit to dwell in our hearts?) These questions are mutually supplementary; no one can be deduced from both or either of the other two. They arise not only from the confession that the God who reveals Himself in Scripture is Triune but also from the conclusion of our preceding philosophical analysis, viz., that the question of God's existence must be discussed within all three modes of being. By approaching Christian doctrine in this new way we shall learn why the Sabbath should be a primary doctrinal theme, discover why Jesus is "the God who is God-man," see why the incarnation could only have occurred by means of the virgin birth, and find a reason for confessing the Holy Spirit to be God in person. Thereby we fulfill the purpose of doctrinal theology. This purpose is to present the affirmations of revelation in such a way that their intrinsic connections and reasons are clearly displayed.

V

Toward an American Theology

SECULARIZATION AND SPIRITUALIZATION

Dietrich Bonhoeffer, the patron saint of secular Christianity, observed that European secularization and American secularization reflect opposed tendencies.[1] In European secularization, religion ceases to exist as a separate phenomenon because the state, science, commerce, and other secular institutions are invested with autonomous dignity and power until they finally encompass the full meaning of life. In American secularization, religion ceases to exist as a separate phenomenon because it seeks to embody itself fully in the state, science, business, and other worldly institutions by identifying its concerns wholly with theirs. American secularization, Bonhoeffer notes, originates in the spiritual, or enthusiastic, conception of the state and society, "whose destiny it is to be taken up into the Church even on this earth."[2] Hence, there is this difference: in the European context "secularization" means the vanquishing of the spiritual by the worldly; in the American context it means the engulfing of the worldly within the spiritual. In both kinds of secularization the Church, as a separate institution, loses its unique function. But in Europe the Church ceases to exist because "the world comes of age" and no longer needs it; in America, the Church ceases to exist because it fully embodies its spirit in all the other institutions of life.

[1] Dietrich Bonhoeffer, *No Rusty Swords,* E. Robertson, ed. (New York, 1965), p. 108.
[2] *Ibid.*

[108]

Rather than persist in an equivocal use of the term "secularization" to indicate these two differing processes, and rather than adopt a purely formal device to distinguish them (e. g., "secularization¹" and "secularization²"), I suggest that we follow Bonhoeffer's *interpretation* of this phenomenon and speak of European "secularization" and American "spiritualization." For, as Bonhoeffer notes, the peculiar form of American secularization originates in the claim of Puritans and spiritualists "to be building the kingdom of God publicly and visibly."³ And it is because Europe drove out these groups who sought to create an ideal society in this world that she deprived herself of the spiritualistic alternative to secularization.

The Puritan and spiritualist program to create a righteous society in history (i. e., establish the kingdom of God) is usually called "theocracy." Theocracy seeks to attain God's kingdom in this world, not the next. This is the fundamental theme of religion in America.

Because of its concentration on God and His kingdom, American Christianity has tended to reduce the Reformation concentration on human sin and Jesus Christ the Redeemer to a secondary emphasis. When, as in Reformation theology, human sin and the need for redemption are made primary emphases, the kingdom of God must be a secondary emphasis—for the very possibility of attaining that kingdom in this world must be denied. Moreover, to focus on sin and man's need for redemption forces a theology to make Jesus Christ, as Redeemer, the primary religious symbol. But in American Christianity, this Reformation emphasis on the symbol of "the cross of Christ" is never primary. Bonhoeffer notes just this characteristic when he says that American Christianity is "still essentially religion and ethics. But because of this, the person and work of Jesus Christ must, for theology, sink into the background . . . because it is not recognized as the sole ground of radical judgment [on sin] and radical forgiveness."⁴

It is striking that Bonhoeffer—in spite of his appreciation of the social and political strengths of American Christianity—shows no comparable appreciation of it as a *theological* reality. For example, he is satisfied to understand American Christianity by means of historical and sociological explanations: Europe drove out the spiritualists, and so these groups now exercise a disproportionate forma-

³ *Ibid.*, p. 108.
⁴ *Ibid.*, pp. 117 f.

tive influence on American religion today. He does not ask whether the theology of these spiritualists might be correct; such theology is, he says again and again, sheer utopianism and idolatry. Hence Bonhoeffer can pronounce the ethnocentric judgment that "God has granted American Christianity no Reformation."[5]

Bonhoeffer's judgment is ethnocentric because he uses different criteria in comparing religion in America with European Christianity. He explains American religion *sociologically*, but he explains his own German religion *theologically*. According to Bonhoeffer, Martin Luther was a reforming prophet through whom God granted the gift of the "Reformation of the Church of Jesus Christ by the Word of God"; in contrast, however, the spiritualists came to America not because of the providence of God, but because they were driven out by the Europeans (i.e., by those who were in large part adherents to God's "Reformation").[6] Suppose, however, we were to utilize Bonhoeffer's technique and simply reverse the criteria, interpreting the European Reformation *sociologically* and American Christianity *theologically*. Then we might say that the Reformation was not primarily a religious event, but was merely the accidental result of social and psychological circumstances: the rise of nationalism and capitalism, the renaissance of learning, the immorality and superstition of late medieval Christianity, and the volatile temper of the Wittenberg monk. But, as if snatching a remnant from this conflagration, God carried His new Israel to these shores, a free and democratic people whose trust in divine providence and whose theocratic hope are evidences that the true Church of Jesus Christ has been reestablished here.

I offer such an obviously fallacious comparison in order to show the inadequacy of Bonhoeffer's similar device. In fact, of course, both sociological and theological factors must be considered in any fair comparison between European and American Christianity. However, it is difficult to encourage such a comparison because of the widespread prejudice that American Christianity has no indigenous theology.[7] It seems clear, for example, that Bonhoeffer makes this assump-

---

[5] *Ibid.*, p. 117.

[6] *Ibid.*, p. 102.

[7] Ernst Benz suggests that two prejudices govern European judgments regarding American Christianity. "The first prejudice is: *Americana non leguntur*—'one does not read American literature,' in this case, theological literature. The second prejudice is: 'There is no independent American theology.' " *Evolution and Christian Hope*, H. Frank, trans. (New York, 1966), p. 143.

tion. The only "real" theologians he finds in America are those who are reiterating European doctrine.[8] All else is, at best, a pagan humanism, and at worst an eclectic and inconsistent conglomeration of sectarian oddities and spiritualistic wrongheadedness. Because of this view of the matter, Bonhoeffer never seems to contemplate the possibility that American theology might raise specific theological objections to certain of the positions of the Reformation or Counter Reformation.

I suggest, however, that American Christianity is not a conglomeration of inconsistencies, but is a full and balanced interpretation of ecumenical Christian faith. Hence I believe that it is possible to understand American Christianity theologically and to compare it, on this point, with the European religious tradition. Moreover, when this is done, we shall be forced to make a judgment about the relative adequacy of these two traditions, and we shall see, at that time, why it is necessary to acknowledge that there are fundamental defects in the traditional western interpretation of the Christian faith. These defects are not to be found so much in *what* this tradition teaches as in *how* it teaches these things. That is, many of its emphases are wrong, and some essential themes are therefore omitted altogether. We shall see, for example, that western European Christianity places a disproportionate emphasis on the New Testament, especially the Pauline writings, and therefore fails to give an adequate place to Old Testament teaching. It ascribes to the doctrine of sin a centrality that leads to a distorted understanding of the person and work of Jesus Christ. Its norms for understanding human life are drawn primarily from a theory of nature rather than from an understanding of the world as God's creation. It has displaced the Trinity from its proper place in the life of faith. It has neglected the work of the Holy Spirit and the communal life of the Church as God's present kingdom.

Many of these criticisms of western European theology will not be made here for the first time. They have been made previously by both Eastern Orthodoxy and Judaism. Therefore, I acknowledge from the outset a resemblance which many European commentators have also mentioned: that American Christianity shares with Judaism

[8] "True, it cannot be denied that the dangers which thus threaten contemporary American Christianity are clearly seen by some leading theologians. Reinhold and Richard Niebuhr, Pauck, Miller and many others of the younger generation continue to speak in a *reformed* way." Bonhoeffer, *op. cit.*, p. 117. (My italics.)

its theocratic emphasis and that, in the last analysis, its spiritualistic interpretation of the Christian faith in terms of worship and incarnation (rather than sin and crucifixion) binds American religion more closely to Orthodoxy than to the western Church. For these reasons, we cannot accept the assumption of European theologians that either the Reformation or the Counter Reformation should stand as a norm over the theology we undertake today.

THE SABBATH AS SACRAMENT

What I am about to undertake in the remainder of this chapter is the construction of a normative doctrinal system that will exhibit the characteristic emphases of American Christianity as a full and balanced interpretation of divine revelation. By calling this a "construction," I acknowledge that no such thing as a systematic American theology has yet been developed. But I believe that the elements for it already exist and can be exhibited as a system, if they are ordered in terms of the single perspective they presuppose, and if certain doctrinal lacunae are filled by drawing proper implications. The fundamental perspective, as I have mentioned above, is the American vision of holy worldliness, the sanctification of all things by the Holy Spirit. It has frequently been noted that American Christianity is preoccupied with the Holy Spirit: America is the cradle of Pentecostalism and the adopted homeland of religious utopianism.[9] Such social movements are only the more exotic exhibitions of a tendency that has permeated even those denominations that self-consciously trace their lineage back to the continent.

The goal of my undertaking, therefore, is to show that God's end in creation is the sanctification, or spiritualization, of the world. But the reflection by which we shall attain this goal begins with quite a different topic. We shall first take up another peculiarly American religious phenomenon: the Puritan Sabbath, that day of rest so scrupulously observed by our forefathers. What can this peculiar rite, which seems to modern man to embody all those religious tendencies that are antiworldly, have to do with the holy worldliness of the kingdom of God?

It is one of the peculiarities of Christian history that the American Puritans attempted to reestablish an institution which the Church, in

[9] John Nichol, *Pentecostalism* (New York, 1966), esp. ch. 3.

its continuing opposition to Judaism, had rejected. There is, of course, an obvious basis for Christian observance of the Sabbath. The commandment to keep the Sabbath holy is included in the Decalogue and would seem, therefore, to be part of the universal moral law that is binding on all men. Yet because of anti-Jewish polemics, Christian theologians have generally argued that the Sabbath commandment is not like the other nine, but only established a "ceremony" that Jesus Christ later abolished. In this way they have denied that keeping the Sabbath is one aspect of general human righteousness. Augustine, for example, argued that the commandments of the Decalogue are "written by God himself in the hearts of men by the presence of the Holy Spirit, who sheds abroad in our hearts the love which is the fulfilling of the law."[10] But he is quick to add that only nine of the Ten Commandments are so written; the Holy Spirit does not write the commandment of the Sabbath on our hearts. Therefore, according to Augustine, who represents the dominant Christian tradition, the Holy Spirit is not the Spirit of Sabbath holiness. Yet, as we shall see, this is not true. The Holy Spirit is the Spirit of the Sabbath. For this reason, God's establishment of the Sabbath reveals His ultimate purpose for His creation: namely, the sanctification of all things. This theological teaching has not, of course, been utterly neglected by all theologians before the Puritans. For example, Hugh of St. Victor, a twelfth-century theologian whose writings later influenced Calvin, specifically relates the Sabbath to the Holy Spirit by pointing out the eschatological character of this day:

Whoever in the present life shall keep this Sabbath so as to consent to no evil will arrive in the future life at that eternal Sabbath of God where he will perceive no evil just as was said: "And there shall be month after month, and Sabbath after Sabbath" [Isa. 66:23]. Thus that precept seems to refer specially to the person of the Holy Spirit when it is said: "Keep holy the Sabbath day," that we may indeed accept Him in the present and . . . possess Him in the future unto the joy of life.[11]

Now, in fact, the Old Testament does contain two different explanations of the meaning of the Sabbath, one of which could be understood to support the view that it is a ceremony peculiar to the

[10] St. Augustine, "On the Spirit and the Letter," P. Holmes, trans., *Basic Writings of St. Augustine,* W. Oates, ed. (New York, 1948), I, ch. 36, p. 488.

[11] Hugh of St. Victor, *On the Sacraments of the Christian Faith,* R. Deferrari, trans., I.12.8 (Cambridge, Mass., 1951), p. 195 f.

Jews. In the Deuteronomic version of the Decalogue, the Sabbath is presented as a remembrance of the slavery of the Jews in Egypt and a celebration of their own national redemption—a redemption that has, in Christianity, been supplanted by the crucifixion and resurrection of Jesus Christ. The Deuteronomic justification of the commandment to do no work on the Sabbath is as follows: "You shall remember that you were a servant in the land of Egypt, and the Lord your God brought you out thence with a mighty hand and an outstretched arm; therefore the Lord your God commanded you to keep the sabbath day" (Deut. 5:15).

Much contemporary theological interpretation of the Old Testament seems to assume this Deuteronomic explanation of the Sabbath as decisive. That is, the Sabbath commandment is regarded not as a natural, or moral, law but as a positive law originating in the history of a particular people, and therefore binding only upon them. It is, so to say, a peculiar national ceremony—something like the Fourth of July. The observance of such a national holiday is binding only upon citizens of a particular nation. Such is the view of those theologians who assert God acts only in history and never in nature. They hold that the Sabbath celebrates God's redemptive work, and they regard the alternative explanation of the Sabbath as a "law of nature" which is morally binding on all men as a later paganizing (or at least, secondary ontologizing) of Israel's true historical faith.

The Puritans, on the other hand, regarded just this alternative understanding of the Sabbath as a law of nature, or a law of creation binding upon all men, as the correct one. This alternative understanding is based, of course, on the first chapters of Genesis; it is also given as the justification for the Sabbath commandment in the Exodus version of the Decalogue: ". . . for in six days the Lord made heaven and earth, the sea, and all that is in them, and rested the seventh day; therefore the Lord blessed the sabbath day and hallowed it" (Ex. 20:11).

This explanation of the commandment must be interpreted as implying that the Sabbath is binding not only upon Israel, but also upon all other creatures. It is not, therefore, intended as a ceremony that is the basis for a continuing separation of Israel from the nations. Rather, it is in the same category as the commandment not to murder: i.e., it is a universal moral law.

Critical historical inquiry concerning the chronological relation of the two biblical explanations of the Sabbath commandment cannot decide which of the two is theologically fundamental. According to the canon of Scripture, the "creation interpretation" of the Sabbath is affirmed to be theologically prior to the "redemption interpretation." This means, therefore, that the Sabbath commandment is always binding upon all men—whether they obey it or not! In the redemption of Israel from Egypt, the Sabbath is not established for the first time, but is reestablished; the moral law is not first published at Sinai, but is republished there. Hence, because the law of the Sabbath is grounded in the order of creation itself and pertains to all creatures, the traditional Christian interpretation of the Sabbath as a ceremony now abolished by Jesus Christ is incorrect. The Puritans were right.

The conflict between the creation and the redemption interpretations of the Sabbath does not concern simply the scope of the commandment, but also the character of the day itself. The "creation interpretation" not only regards Sabbath observance as something required of all men, but also assumes that the day is qualitatively different from all other days. For in Genesis, the Sabbath "rest" is not defined by contrasting it with man's work; rather it is defined as something primarily appropriate to God. The "redemption interpretation" of Sabbath "rest," on the other hand, defines it as the opposite of man's work; that is, "rest" is a man's abstinence from the work he does on the other six days. On this view of the matter, "holiness" is the opposite of "worldliness"; it is a "separation." And by this separation the Sabbath is essentially bound up with chronology.

In the "creation interpretation" of the Sabbath, however, the chronological contrast between two times of man seems secondary. The Genesis chronology is basically a literary device used to point out a certain hierarchy of being. Whatever comes "later" is "higher." So considered, the days of Genesis show the teleological ordering of created life toward God. The "days" of creation are steps which rise from the day and night to the earth and waters to the plants and animals and on to man. Man, as the last creature formed by God, is also the highest creature; to him is given the right of dominion over every other created thing. All other creatures are less than man from the point of view of what is technically called "dignity": they are all created for his sake and ordered to his good.

However, even though man is the highest of all the beings in "nature" (i. e., all that is created in the first six days), Genesis teaches

I

that God establishes yet one more dimension in the world to be higher than man himself. This is the Sabbath Day. Just as man is intended by God to have dominion over all other creatures, so the Sabbath Day is established so that it might have dominion over him. It is the good which man is made to serve, the end apart from which his life will fail to find its true use. For just as the land and its vegetation and animal life are good in themselves, but find their proper ordering in serving the good of man, so man is good in himself, but finds the chief and proper use of his life when he serves the holiness of the Sabbath. For man is made for Sabbath holiness. His end is not in himself, but in the holiness of God which, through the Sabbath, is established in the world as the final joy of all created things.

We are so habituated today to a negative understanding of Sabbath rest as an abstinence from all those activities usually associated with human fulfillment that this alternative way of conceiving Sabbath rest as the enjoyment of holiness may seem strange to us. Moreover, the modern world is so committed to the view that man's greatest good is his own fulfillment that it may even seem inhuman to suggest that God has made man for a still greater end: namely, that he glorify God by keeping the Sabbath holy. The very suggestion that man is not the measure of all things, but is ordered within a hierarchy that moves toward God, may seem to denigrate the ultimacy of created things and be offensive to contemporary humanists. But such a vision of the Sabbath as a sacrament revealing a dimension of holy goodness higher than any human goodness did not seem repressive to the Puritans, nor even to those who—while denying the Puritan doctrine of sin—still held fast to their vision. Consider, for example, these words of Ralph Waldo Emerson, the climax of his address to the senior class at the Harvard Divinity School in 1838:

Two inestimable advantages Christianity has given us; first, the Sabbath, the jubilee of the whole world; whose light dawns welcome alike into the closet of the philosopher, into the garret of toil, and into prison cells, and everywhere suggests, even to the vile, the dignity of spiritual being. Let it stand forevermore, a temple, which new love, new faith, new sight shall restore to more than its first splendor to mankind. And secondly, the institution of preaching—the speech of man to man—essentially the most flexible of all organs, or all forms. What hinders that now, everywhere, in pulpits, in lecture-rooms, in houses, in fields, wherever the invitation of men or your own occasion lead you, you speak the very truth, as your life and conscience teach it, and cheer the waiting, fainting hearts of men with new hope and new revelation?[12]

In these words, Emerson presents a positive understanding of the Sabbath as the revelation of the highest dimension of reality, "the dignity of spiritual being." How little such a view has to do with mere chronology, separation, and abstinence! Rather, it reveals a preoccupation with the chief end of creation, a concern with the ultimate purpose of all life. And, I believe, just such a metaphysical vision of the holy jubilee of the world is implicit also in the Puritan conviction that the Sabbath is no minor article of religion, but a key to the whole of life—its very sacrament. This vision is the new perspective characteristic of American Christianity, a perspective that will lead eventually to a new interpretation of all the traditional articles of faith.

Precisely at this point, where the Christian religion shifts its fundamental concern from redemption to sanctification within the world, it discovers its kinship with Judaism. In Judaism, too, the fundamental sacrament of life is the Sabbath, a day that reveals the eschaton in space and time, "the jubilee of the whole world." In Judaism, too, there is the same positive view of Sabbath holiness as the presence of God in the world. For example, Abraham Joshua Heschel asserts that "while Jewish tradition offers us no definition of the concept of eternity, it tells us how to experience the taste of eternity or eternal life within time."[13] And he recalls the legend that

. . . at the time when God was giving the Torah to Israel, He said to them: My children! If you accept the Torah and observe my mitzvot, I will give you for all eternity a thing most precious that I have in my possession.

—And what, asked Israel, is that precious thing which Thou wilt give us if we obey Thy Torah?

—The world to come.

—Show us in this world an example of the world to come.

—The Sabbath is an example of the world to come.[14]

In American Puritanism, as in Judaism, the Sabbath is regarded as the exemplar of the world to come. In fact, in American religion,

[12] "The Divinity School Address," *Three Prophets of Religious Liberalism*, C. C. Wright, ed. (Boston, 1961), p. 111 f.
[13] Abraham Joshua Heschel, *The Sabbath* (Cleveland, 1963), p. 74.
[14] *Ibid.*, p. 73.

the Sabbath replaces the Christological sacraments characteristic of European Christianity: a single eschatological sacrament replaces the two traditional sacraments that focus the religious life on sin and redemption (i. e., baptism and the Lord's Supper). The perceptive reader may have already sensed that Emerson's statement above actually involves a new conception of the "marks" of the true Church. In European Protestantism, the marks of the Church include preaching and administration of the Christological sacraments. But with Emerson the marks of true Christianity are preaching and the Sabbath. This new sacrament of American Christianity is not *Christological,* but *theological.* It focuses not upon the death of Christ but upon the theocracy of God, who is sanctifying His creation through His providential works.

The fundamental change in theological perspective that has occurred within American Christianity can be expressed as the substitution of a new question for the old one: Rather than asking, "How can I find a gracious God?" or "What shall I do to be saved?" the American asks, "What is the purpose of God's providence?" or "Why did God create the world?" For, as we have seen above, concern with the Sabbath as a law of creation suggests a theocentric rather than anthropocentric orientation: the activities of man's life (his "work") are understood to be ordered toward the holiness and worship of God. As the old Puritan formula expressed this insight, "The chief end of man is to glorify God and enjoy him forever."

This theocratic orientation can be expressed formally as concern with the question *cur creatio*: "Why did God create the world?" Such a concern contrasts sharply with the western theological concern with the question *cur deus homo:* "Why did God become man?" In what follows, therefore, we shall consider what happens to our theological understanding of Jesus Christ when we subordinate *"cur deus homo"* to *"cur creatio."* And we shall see how, by subordinating this Christological question to the question about God's purpose in creation, American Christianity is able to develop a system of doctrine which does full justice to the work and person of the Holy Spirit— a problem never satisfactorily resolved within the perspective of western theology. Through this method of investigation, we shall discover an intrinsic theological relation between the Sabbath practices so characteristic of early America and the later, equally characteristic, Pentecostal and utopian movements.

HOLINESS, THE GLORY OF GOD

Let us recall that, in this chapter, I am attempting to construct a system of doctrine capable of exhibiting the characteristic emphases of American Christianity as a balanced and true expression of Christian faith. My argument is not, therefore, intended as historical. In the last section, of course, I stressed the Puritan and post-Puritan concern with the Sabbath; however, my intention there and henceforth is not to present a description of American Christianity, but to explore the theological possibilities implicit within its unique starting point: the question *cur creatio* and its answer "the Sabbath." Moreover, I believe this starting point is right, not because our ancestors began here, but because it adequately expresses the unifying perspective within Scripture itself. For the origin of an idea may affect its relevance, but it never determines its truth.

Now, in fact, keeping the Sabbath holy is nothing other than the way that a man lives to the glory of God. For Sabbath holiness and the glory of God are one and the same thing. I grant that this equation is not an obvious one. It involves a special conception of holiness, one that identifies holiness with God himself; for only if "holiness = God" will "living for holiness = living for God alone." In this section, therefore, I shall analyze various notions of holiness until we come to the one that is consistent with the idea of the Sabbath I have presented above. There are, of course, certain understandings of holiness that are inconsistent with the idea of a Sabbath Day; but when we find the one that is consistent, then we shall see why the holiness of the Sabbath is nothing other than the glory of God. By approaching the idea of the glory of God by this "back door," so to say, we shall come to appreciate the peculiar doctrinal emphasis on divine glory that is at the heart of American religion.

a. Holiness as a Communicable Property. Holiness may be understood as a characteristic proper to God but also communicable to other beings. Such a view of it is found both in primitive religions and in modern theologies. In primitive religions, holiness is often understood as a kind of substance which can be transmitted through a causal nexus (e.g., by touch or by utterance). It can adhere to creatures and thereby divinize them, for the addition of holiness to any created nature transforms or even transubstantiates it. Once "divinized," the creature is no longer suited to fulfill its natural functions. It is "set apart" for holy purposes, and possesses divine power to destroy or to make alive. There are reminders of this primitive notion of holiness in the Bible: for example, the displacement of the natural faculties of speech in prophets possessed by the Spirit, or in the power of the Ark of the Covenant to strike dead all those who touch it with profane hands. Moreover, the conception of holiness as a communicable attribute of God is presupposed in many popular views of prayer and the sacraments, healing waters, relics, and so forth.

However, it is not only characteristic of primitive and popular religion to conceive holiness as a communicable substance. Certain modern theologies of history also predicate holiness of the creature, e. g., of political causes and social groups. In these theologies, holiness effects a kind of political transubstantiation, bestowing upon a given cause or group absolute saving power. Such a "holy group" (e. g., the Marxist "proletariat") is beyond finite criticism. Just as the Ark of the Covenant was made of wood, but was viewed as the substantive vessel of divine holiness, so a political group or cause may be unjust or destructive and yet be regarded as God's own holy power present in the world. No criticism can count against such a claim; its basis is sheer fath. Later in this chapter we shall consider further examples of this point of view—especially the notion of the *Übermensch* ("superman").

b. Holiness as an Incommunicable Attribute. The strong biblical opposition to idolatry implies a rejection of the idea that holiness is a communicable attribute of God. Scripture opposes both the superstitions of primitive religion and those modern theologies that impute holiness to particular political causes or groups. Following this scriptural teaching, Christian theology has generally defined holiness as an incommunicable property of God. It is incommunicable —i. e., God cannot share it in common with any other being—since it is what makes Him "God." Holiness is the defining characteristic of the Godhead.

Traditional Christian theology has, however, sometimes spoken of holiness as an incommunicable property of God's *nature* (or essence). It is thought to resemble God's eternity or His omnipotence, two characteristics that also seem to belong to God alone. There are, however, certain difficulties with this view. It would seem, first of all, that the very notion of an incommunicable nature is self-contradictory—for the concept of a nature (or essence) was developed in order to account for characteristics that are common to many beings. Something that can be characteristic of only one being would therefore seem to be no essence at all, but something proper to its unique existence. But this is not always the case.

The concept of an incommunicable nature is meaningful whenever we are thinking about characteristics that are not common *in fact,* but might be common *in principle.* For example, the nature of a dodo bird is common (or communicable) to two or more such birds in principle; but the nature of the last living dodo bird was incommunicable in fact. There seems to be no reason why God might not be conceived to have attributes that are incommunicable in just this sense. Consider, for example, the argument between the Augustinians and the Thomists regarding God's eternity: the Augustinians asserted that God alone is eternal in principle; the Thomists found nothing in principle to exclude the contention that a plurality of other beings might also have existed eternally—whether such beings actually did exist or not. From the Thomist perspective, to suppose that eternal creatures exist does not create theological problems—for "eternity" is not the *definiens* of God. A second example: Jonathan Edwards found nothing in principle against the notion that there might be many omniscient beings, for he correctly saw that omniscience is not God's defining characteristic. Finally, we can apply this conceptual distinction to a contemporary problem by considering the possibility that scientists will soon create life: some persons contend that God will be disproved as soon as biologists create living protein molecules in a test tube. But this is not the case. For the mere fact that God alone has created life in the past does not mean that Christians are committed to the view that this characteristic is incommunicably His in principle. That is, "creativity" might be unique to God *in fact,* at the present time; but this does not mean that such a property could not in principle be possessed by other beings, nor does it mean that men will never, in fact, be creators of life.

According to Scripture, however, holiness is not incommunicably God's in fact, but in principle. This is why Scripture defines idolatry as sin, since idolatry claims holiness for one who is not God. Holiness is not, therefore, like eternity, omniscience, or creativity—characteristics that may in fact belong only to God even though they do not constitute His definiens. It is something else. But for just this reason, it is unsatisfactory to think of holiness as an incommunicable attribute of God's *nature*. For the concept of a nature that is incommunicable in principle is meaningless—since the concept "nature" (or "essence") was formulated in order to account for characteristics that can in principle be common.

c. Holiness as God's Very Existence. The argument against conceiving holiness is to be an incommunicable attribute of God's nature suggests that holiness might better be understood as *God's very existence.* For existence is one, i. e., it is unique and incommunicable. And the concept of "existence" symbolizes that which is incommunicable. Certain modern religious scholars, especially those who follow Rudolf Otto, understand holiness in this way. Holiness is not, they say, a quality; rather it is a being. The term "holy" should not be used as an adjective ("the holy God") but as a noun ("The Holy"). The term "holiness" is, therefore, misleading—for it suggests that the term "holy" is an adjective. ("Holiness" is like "redness"— a nominative paronym that presupposes a primary adjectival form, viz., "holy" or "red.")

According to Otto's view, "The Holy" is the personal name of God. But such a contention implies that God is wholly other and that there is an utter discontinuity between Him and the world. For "The Holy" is a being so unlike other beings that "He" cannot coexist with them in the same time and space. Were a man to encounter "The Holy," he would have to cease being a man—transcending himself, perhaps, by "ecstatic reason" (Tillich). Or, if by chance "The Holy" were to appear to men in the world, then it would annihilate them, overwhelming the spatiotemporal order in which they live (Otto). For there can be no relation between beings unless they are similar qua beings; therefore, there can be no relation between "The Holy" and a person. The most powerful proponent of this view of "The Holy" (with its concomitant antipersonalism) is Paul Tillich. He uses this idea of God to undergird his "Protestant protest" against every claim that holiness is communicated to a created reality.

It should be clear that such a concept of "The Holy" is theologically invalid. It renders any adequate understanding of the Sabbath impossible. "The Holy" cannot enter time and space, and man qua man can never have communion with "The Holy." Moreover, in Chapter III I suggested my own philosophical criticism of this concept. The All-encompassing Whole of reality is God; but this Whole is a being in exactly the same sense that all other beings are beings. That is, it is one. God is "The Holy One." To say that the God is holy is not to say that He is a peculiar kind of being; it is to ascribe a unique property to Him, a property that He cannot in principle share in common with any other being. We do not have a categorical distinction available to describe such a unique property. Modern philosophy has neglected this dimension of reality. I shall therefore suggest a new term for specifying the unique property of a person, or existence: the category of "dignity." Holiness refers neither to *essence* (i. e., to an attribute of God's nature) nor to *existence* (i. e., to God's very being); rather it is a *dignity*.

d. Holiness as God's Dignity or Glory. Let us attempt to understand the meaning of "dignity" by considering a Hebrew concept which is similar to it, the concept of *kabod* (usually translated as "glory"). The *kabod* of God is not His nature, or essence; it does not define what God is. Nor is God's *kabod* His very existence, for the word *kabod* cannot be used as a proper name. Rather, God's *kabod* is the weightiness, heaviness, degree, or dignity proper to His being who He is. Qua being, God is only one among many; qua essence, God is what He is—an eternal, wise, and free being; qua dignity (*kabod*), however, God surpasses all other being in degree and worth and weight.

I shall attempt to clarify the notion of dignity by discussing it in relation to three different problems. (1) Dignity is the basis of authority. It is what gives weight to words, i. e., turns them into commands. (2) Dignity is the basis of tragedy. It is what gives life importance and redeems it from triviality. (3) Dignity is the basis of meaning. It is not identical with meaning, since meaning is related to essence and is grasped by understanding. Even though life may have meaning, it may not have dignity. It is in conjunction with this third problem that we shall consider certain limitations in Paul Tillich's interpretation of religion.

1. God's *kabod* is the basis of His authority. His holiness is what makes Him God and gives Him the right to command worship and obedience. His intrinsic dignity gives His words weight, gives them the right to be heard, gives them their power and authority. A theocratic theology, which focuses on the sovereign government of God over His world, must be a theology of holiness. That is, it must understand God's commands to be rooted in His holiness, in His

right to command. If it does not do this, but rather establishes God's authority in His mere power (an attribute of nature), then a theocratic theology becomes demonic. Authority is not the same as the possession of sheer power, for authority rests upon a personal dignity that gives to judgments an intrinsic weight and worth. Because it rests upon dignity and not on sheer power, authority is always legitimate. To call authority "illegitimate" is to imply that it is really not authoritative. This is the case with respect to both institutional authority and the noninstitutional authority of such individuals as Jesus, who spoke "with authority." Max Weber has called this non-institutional authority "charismatic." Charisma is derived from a person's dignity or *kabod*.

Since authority is found both in heaven and on earth, dignity is not a concept that is applicable to God alone. Every person may have dignity—though only God's dignity is constituted by holiness. Dignity is a formal notion, and its material content can vary from case to case. A learned judge has *kabod*; so does a monarch. A man receives *kabod* from a good wife, and children may bring honor and glory to their parents. There can be no doubt that dignity is a crucial factor in the functioning of all human life. The neglect of this factor by modern thinkers leaves great gaps in our understanding of the world.

2. We can also clarify the idea of dignity by recalling Aristotle's suggestion that a genuine tragedy must concern a person of intrinsic importance, or weight. Why is this the case? If the dramatic protagonist has no dignity, then whatever he does or whatever happens to him will not be of significance to anyone at all. (In fact, if he lacks all sense of his own personal dignity, then he will not even care what happens to himself—a phenomenon found in both modern drama and in modern life.) Dignity bestows importance upon life. Only an important calamity is truly tragic. This is why, for example, the death of our president was so overwhelming a tragedy and why, conversely, the death of a totally unknown person (if there were such a being) would not be tragic at all.

We can contrast Aristotle's suggestion that tragedy depends upon dignity with the modern theory that claims tragedy depends upon meaning. Lionel Abel, for example, argues that no dramatic tragedy is written today because men no longer have any sense of the overall meaning of life. His proposal is very different from the view of Aristotle, who saw that meaning is not a sufficient condition of tragedy

—for there may be meaning to life, but there can be no tragedy unless that meaning is important. Consider, for example, the *Death of a Salesman*. This drama is not truly tragic, for Willy Loman has no dignity; nothing he does and nothing that happens to him has weight. In the last analysis, his death is pathetic, but hardly important enough to be tragic. From these and other considerations, I believe that dignity is both different from and more fundamental than meaning.

3. We can carry the analysis one step further by contrasting my proposal that dignity is more fundamental than meaning with the view of Paul Tillich. According to Tillich, the problem of modern man is his feeling that life is meaningless. But is this truly the case? Is it not rather that, even when modern men do see the meaning of life, they do not necessarily regard it as important? For example, consider the man who works on a production line. Some social critics suggest that his boredom arises from the fact that he does not understand how his small work contributes to making the total finished product; if he understood this, his problems would be solved. (The argument is illustrated by reference to the days when "whole men" made "whole things.") However, it is not the case that simply because men see the meaning of their lives, or see their essential contribution to the life of the whole society or cosmos, they will therefore feel their lives are important. Meaningfulness alone does not bestow importance upon life, nor give it tragic proportions. Only dignity does this.

To conclude, we can now see why the space and time of the Sabbath is not *empty* even though God rested and did not create any new beings or any new meaning on this day. By His mere presence in this opening in time, God bestows holiness upon the world, i. e., an importance proportionate to His own *kabod*. This is why Emerson speaks of the Sabbath's suggesting to man "the dignity of spiritual being," and why Calvin describes the chief end of man as the *kabod*, or glory, of God.

At the beginning of this section, I suggested that an understanding of Sabbath holiness would also help us understand why holiness must be regarded as the glory of God. By considering the biblical opposition to idolatry, we have seen that holiness should be ascribed to God as incommunicable. By considering the biblical teaching on the Sabbath as the presence of God to man within space and time, we have seen that holiness cannot be a unique kind of "being": God is not "The Holy," rather, He is "The Holy One." The term "holy" designates a dignity of God's person, necessarily incommunicable. Hence, wherever there is holiness, God is personally present—for there can be no communication of holiness from one person to another. God can communicate His wisdom or freedom to a creature without being personally present in or to that creature (just as a teacher can communicate knowledge to a student without being personally present with or in that student). But God cannot communicate the dignity of His person to others, although He may let them enjoy His holiness when He is present with or in them. (So Israel is called "a holy people" because God has chosen to dwell in her midst.)

Since, therefore, God created the world for Sabbath holiness, He must personally enter the world and dwell therein. The mere time and space of the Sabbath is the formal and material precondition for God's personal coming. By His personal coming God sanctifies the Sabbath. The Sabbath is, so to say, the world's aptitude for the incarnation. And it is to this question of God's Sabbath presence in the world that we now turn.

"GOD WITH US" AND "GOD FOR US"

The argument I have thus far developed has taken up two characteristic elements in American Christianity, Sabbath observance and the theme of the glory of God, and has shown that there is an intrinsic theological relation between them. Moreover, I have suggested that this doctrinal-sacramental complex implies a perspective that continues to shape American religion even though the peculiarities of Puritanism per se have long since been abandoned. This perspective may be described as theocratic—a striving to have God's purpose for creation actually be realized in the world—a desire to actualize eschatological holiness in space and time. Such a perspective implies that the fundamental theological question is *cur creatio*.

I have already indicated that to accept the theocratic perspective is to put all theological reflection about the meaning of Jesus Christ into a framework. In this way, we do not begin theology with Christology, much less reduce it to Christology. That is, we do not do theology in the manner of Barth, Bultmann, or Bonhoeffer. Rather, we allow our answers to the question *cur creatio* to guide our reflection on

Jesus Christ. This means, of course, that Christology will be the second rather than the first topic in the doctrinal system.

To make Christology second, according to Bonhoeffer, pushes it "into the background." This judgment is repeated again and again by theologians who oppose a *theologia crucis* to a *theologia gloriae* —as if a theology of glory were intrinsically incapable of doing full justice to the person and work of Christ. But in fact, only if we take up Christology within a theocratic framework can we affirm the Godhead of Christ and the fullness of His work. The theology of the cross can actually be shown to be a western accommodation to Arianism and naturalism. (Arianism the doctrine that Jesus is not fully God; naturalism the view that regards nature, history, science, and/or philosophy as defining the norms of belief). To make the crucifixion the center of Christian faith is to fix upon the Christological datum that allows the maximum compromise with these two tendencies.

In this section, I shall proceed directly to a theological consideration of the person and purpose of Jesus Christ, introducing historical and descriptive material from American Christianity simply for illustrative purposes. I shall be concerned to show what the Sabbath perspective implies for our understanding of Christ. For whatever it implies ought to be affirmed by American Christianity, and in fact is what American Christianity already tends to affirm (though without the clarity of the theocratic symbols I have discussed above). I shall consider the implications of the Sabbath perspective for the *scope* of Christology (i.e., the purpose for which God was in Christ) and the *form* of Christology (i.e., the manner in which we should understand God to be in Christ).

a. The Scope of Christology. Western theology traditionally defines the purpose of God's activity in Christ as redemption. This is implied by its correlation of the incarnation with the sinfulness of man. If Adam had not sinned, so the argument goes, there would have been no need for the incarnation. From this point of view, since the incarnation is contingent upon the occurrence of sin, the coming of Jesus Christ is understood to be for the sake of our redemption. But this answer to the question *cur deus homo* should be rejected. This does not mean that we should deny that Jesus Christ is our Redeemer, but it does mean that we should not regard His incarnation as contingent upon the occurrence of sin. The incarnation would have occurred whether sin had ever entered the world or not; there-fore its chief reason must be other than redemption.

Western theologians typically charge those who suggest that God would have become incarnate even if sin had not entered into the world with useless hypothesizing. They point out that *in fact* Adam did sin and that *in fact* man is redeemed by the work of the incarnate One. We should not, they argue, speculate about "might have been's." This circumspect warning is quite legitimate. However, it should be pointed out that the "might have been" question has been raised by some theologians not because they wished to speculate about other possible worlds, but because they were attempting to distinguish the primary reason for the incarnation from its secondary reasons. For example, suppose you visit a friend and discover on your arrival at his house that he is moving a heavy trunk. After you have helped him move it, he says, "Thanks for coming over to help me move the trunk." But you had not gone to visit him *for this reason,* even though you were happy to help him with the trunk when you dis-covered his need.

Asking whether God would have become incarnate if Adam had not sinned is like asking whether you would have gone to visit your friend even if he didn't need help. That is, it is a heuristic question, helpful for determining our appropriate response to Jesus Christ. So, for example, if we believe that the chief reason for His incarnation is redemption, then our proper response to Jesus Christ should be gratitude (and this is what some theologians explicitly assert). But if we believe that the chief reason for His incarnation is, say, God's desire to be with us as a friend, then our proper response should be simple enjoyment of friendship with Christ. From this we see that the "might have been" question is not necessarily a useless speculation; rather it can be a serious attempt to cut through secondary issues to the basic terms of the Christian faith. It is an attempt to define the proper character of our response to God's coming.

The advantage in the method developed in this essay, however, is that it avoids inquiring into the primary purpose of Christ's work by means of an hypothetical question. The "might have been" ap-proach to the purpose of the incarnation is inevitable if theology begins with Christology. For then we must ask, "Jesus redeemed us from sin, but what if Adam had not sinned?" Moreover, even asking this heuristic question will never allow us to settle the problem it raises.

What I have suggested, however, is that we avoid this hypothetical approach by first thinking about God's purpose in creating the world; then we can allow our answer to this question to guide our meditations on the incarnation. Rather than entertaining "might have been's," therefore, we shall, in this alternative way, come to understand why the traditional western theory that the essential work of Jesus Christ is redemption is incorrect.

Let us first assume the traditional western position and ask just what Jesus Christ does in His redemptive work. The usual answer to this question is that by His ministry (including His incarnation, crucifixion, and resurrection), He restores the *imago dei,* i.e., He restores whatever it is that made man "man" in the day that God created him. This answer can, of course, also be stated in modern idiom without any change in the essential idea. For example, it may be said that the work of Christ is to "make man truly human" (Lehmann) or to make man "real man" (Ebeling). Such modern expressions intend to affirm that the work of Christ in redemption is to bring men into "maturity" by overcoming whatever prevents them from fulfilling all their natural potentialities. But these theories are false, for they make the chief end of Christ's work less than the chief end of God's work in creating the world. Hence, they are functionally Arian, for it is a theological maxim that the purpose of Christ's work and the purpose of God's work must be one and the same if Jesus Christ is to be fully God. For example, in Athanasius' treatise on the incarnation, the functional identity of Christ's work in redemption with God's work in creation is the basis of ascribing deity to Jesus Christ.[15]

But why is it the case that Christ's work in restoring or actualizing the *imago dei* is less than God's chief end in the creation of the world? The answer is that this pertains to God's intention for the *sixth* day (when He created man in His image) rather than to the Sabbath Day, the chief end of God. Unless the work of Christ fulfills God's Sabbath intention, then it is less than the work of God in creating the world. Not only has western theology failed to recognize this problem, but it has heightened it by setting the sixth day in opposition

[15] "For being the Word of the Father, and above all, he alone of natural fitness was both able to *recreate* everything, and worthy to suffer on behalf of all and to be ambassador for all with the Father." "On the Incarnation of the Word," *Christology of the Later Fathers,* E. Hardy, ed. (Philadelphia, 1954), p. 62. (My italics.)

to the seventh day. How often have we heard that Jesus Christ
abolishes the Sabbath so that men may be truly free! But this suggestion is sheer theological nonsense. The work of Jesus Christ cannot contradict the purpose for which God created the world. To
assert such a contradiction, by explicitly or implicitly opposing the
Sabbath, is to reiterate the old Gnostic claim that the God of the Old
Testament and the God of the New Testament are two different
"Gods."

The scope of Christ's work must be more than redemption (making man truly human or the restoration of the *imago dei*), because
it must be identical with God's purpose in creating the world. The
question *cur deus homo* must be answered not with reference to the
purpose of God for the *sixth* day, but with reference to His purpose
for the Sabbath Day. Only thereby will the purpose of Christ's work
have the same scope as the purpose of God in creating the world.
Now, the Sabbath Day was created by God, so that He Himself might
enter into the world and sanctify it by His personal presence. In this
way, He makes the world holy. And it is this rather than redemption
that is the chief work of Jesus Christ. He is the Lord of the Sabbath,
the one for whom the seventh day was made. The purpose of His
coming, therefore, is simply that He be here. He is not here for the
sake of something else. The presence of the Holy One in our midst
is its own sufficient reason. Nothing exceeds this, for this gives human
life its dignity, worth, and importance. Not the Martha who works,
but the Mary who rests in the presence of God has chosen the "good
portion." For to enjoy God forever is the chief end of man.

Thus, even without adopting their hypothetical manner of arguing,
we see why those theologians who asserted that the incarnation is not
contingent upon the occurrence of sin were correct. The incarnation
proceeds from God's original intention for His creation. God created
the world so that the Sabbath guest, Jesus Christ, might come and
dwell therein. That is, the world was created for the sake of "Eman-
uel, God with us." The incarnation is, therefore, not a rescue operation, decided upon only after sin had entered into the world. Rather,
the coming of Christ fulfills the purpose of God in creating the world.
Sanctification, not redemption, is the chief work of Jesus Christ—
"God with us" rather than "God for us." For this reason, to know
only the benefits of Christ is not to know Christ. To know Christ
only as Redeemer is not to know Christ. To love Christ only with

gratitude because of what He has done or will do for us is not to know Christ. Rather, to know Christ is to enjoy the presence of His person, to take delight in His nearness, to love Him as a friend "being with" whom is its own sufficient reason. Only after we first know Jesus as "God with us" can we truly know Him as "God for us." Only after we know Him as friend can we know Him as Redeemer. The western concentration upon sin and redemption has pushed this correct understanding of the incarnation into the background.

Perhaps the most moving antidote to a distorted understanding of Jesus Christ is found in the writings of Jonathan Edwards, who correctly perceived that our love for Christ should be primarily motivated by a sense of His own intrinsic holiness and dignity rather than by any interest in or existential gratitude for what He might (or might not) have done for us. We should love Jesus for Himself alone rather than for any help He gives us. In a true response to Christ, writes Edwards,

men are affected with the attribute of God's goodness and free grace, not only as it affects their interest, but as a part of the glory and beauty of God's nature. That wonderful and unparalleled grace of God, which is manifested in the work of redemption and shines forth in the face of Jesus Christ is infinitely glorious in itself, and appears so to the angels. . . . This would be glorious whether it were exercized towards us or no. . . . By this sense of the moral beauty of divine things, is understood the sufficiency of Christ as a mediator: for 'tis only by the discovery of the beauty of the moral perfection of Christ, that the believer is let unto knowledge of the excellency of his person, so as to know anything more of it than the devils do: and 'tis only by the knowledge of the excellency of Christ's person, that any know of his sufficiency as a mediator; for the latter depends upon, and rises from the former.[16]

This is the Sabbath vision of American Christianity: that Jesus Christ, "God with us," is intrinsically so holy and attractive that we would love Him for Himself alone even if He were not also our Redeemer.

To stress the priority of "God with us" over "God for us" is not, however, to deny that Jesus is our Redeemer, nor is it to derogate from His redeeming work. Though redemption is a subordinate purpose of His coming, it is essential to the chief end He

[16] Jonthan Edwards, *Religious Affections*, J. Smith, ed. (New Haven, 1959), pp. 248, 273.

K

seeks. Moreover, it was precisely for the sake of our redemption that Jesus Christ endured the cross. But unless we undergird redemption with sanctification, i. e., unless we insist that the sanctification of the world by His mere Sabbath presence is the primary reason Jesus Christ is here, we lack the presupposition that makes His redemptive work worthwhile. For it is clear that unless human life has worth and dignity, there is no necessary reason why anyone should care whether it is redeemed or not.

I suspect that the strong Reformation emphasis on the total corruption of man without a corresponding emphasis upon his dignity has actually undercut what it was intended to support: namely, man's sense that he needs a redeemer. The world agrees that all men are sinners, but it does not see that the redemption of sinners is worth caring about. The relative failure of Christianity to be an effective redemptive force in the world arises in large part from this failure to affirm clearly the spiritual dignity of human life. And, on the other hand, I believe that the power of Judaism to survive in the face of constant enmity and disadvantage arises from its firm sense of being "a holy people," i. e., from its recurring celebration of the Sabbath sacrament. To assert, therefore, that sanctification is the chief reason for the incarnation is not to undercut redemption, but to affirm the sole condition that gives it any meaning.

DYADIC vs. TRIADIC CHRISTOLOGY

We have seen that, from the perspective of the Sabbath commandment, the chief reason for incarnation is not redemption, but sanctification. Jesus Christ is not, first of all, "God for us," but "God with us." To know Jesus Christ, therefore, is not to know His benefits, but to know His person.

There is, of course, a theological reason for insisting that an experience of Jesus Christ as "God with us" requires a knowledge of His very person. For, as we have previously argued, the distinguishing characteristic of God is a property not of His nature, but of His person, viz., holiness. Someone can know things *about God* by knowing characteristics of His nature (e. g., truth or love or happiness). But one can only know God Himself, i. e., know God insofar as He is God, by experiencing the holiness that is the distinguishing property of His existence. Since holiness is inseparable from the person of God, we can only know God in Christ by experiencing Jesus of Nazareth as the Holy One in person.

The assertion that we must experience the person of Jesus as "God with us" is a consequence following from our previous discussion of the Sabbath, the character of holiness, and the scope of incarnation. Yet such an unconditional affirmation that Jesus of Nazareth is God in person implies yet another criticism of western theological tradition. The western Church has refused to grant that the assertion "Jesus is God" tells the essential truth about Him. It has contended, rather, that such an assertion tells only half the truth and must be coupled with the balancing statement that "Jesus is man." To neglect a full truth by consciously affirming only half the truth not only causes confusion, but is even to tell a half-lie. For this reason, the western tradition maintains that the essential truth about Jesus Christ is not that He is "God," but that He is "God-man."

The "God-man" formula was devised by the Church in large part because of its concern to maintain all that is required in order for Jesus to accomplish our redemption. For unless Jesus is like us in all respects, He cannot redeem us in all respects. As the classical maxim stated this relation: whatever He did not assume, He could not raise. The theological concern to affirm the full manhood of Jesus in order to undergird the full reality of His redemptive work has remained, to the present day, the primary support of the God-man formula. Moreover, I believe this concern is correct. Hence my counterproposal that the correct affirmation about Jesus of Nazareth is that He is unconditionally God in person does not intend to reject the "God-man" formula, but to supplement it with another, deeper truth. This supplementary understanding of Jesus is required by the affirmation that sanctification, rather than redemption, is the chief reason for His incarnation. Hence, just as the Sabbath perspective has forced us to revise the traditional understanding of the scope of Christology, it now also forces us to revise the traditional understanding of its form.

b. The Form of Christology. The "God-man" formula of western Christology must be revised, or supplemented, because it does not state in a sufficiently unambiguous way what actual sanctification requires, viz., that the individual person of Jesus of Nazareth be God Himself. This "God-man" formula is a summary of the confession of Chalcedon (451 A.D.), in which the God-manhood of Jesus is understood to mean that He possesses two natures. He is one person (*prosōpon*) who is perfect both in deity (*theotēti*) and in humanity (*anthropōtēti*). Divinity and humanity are ascribed to this one person in equal measure, but nothing is said directly about the person per se. His inner dignity is undefined. Hence, on the Chalcedonian definition, it is possible in principle to regard Jesus as less in person than the Father is in person. That is, the "God-man" formula is open to a "deutero-Arian" interpretation, i.e., an interpretation that ascribes the divine nature, but not the divine dignity, to Jesus.

A deutero-Arian "God-man" formula meets the requirements of the doctrine of redemption (since it ascribes full humanity to Jesus Christ), but it does not meet the requirements of sanctification. For sanctification can occur only if the very person of Jesus is God, i.e., if the property of this individual existence is holiness. (This follows from my earlier discussion of holiness as the glory of God.) Unless Jesus is "The Holy One," He cannot be "God with us" and His presence cannot dignify our lives. And unless Jesus, the babe in the manger, the carpenter of Nazareth, the prophet and healer and crucified One, is God in person, He cannot be the Lord of the Sabbath. But that Jesus is God in person is precisely what the "God-man" formula leaves undetermined. In fact, the tendency of Chalcedon seems against such a notion. For God is not present *in* the very humanity of the God-man; rather, God is present *through* his humanness.

To clarify the difference between God present *in* Jesus' humanness and God present *through* it, let us recall Augustine's interpretation of the two-nature doctrine—an interpretation that is chronologically prior to the formula of Chalcedon and influential in shaping it. According to Augustine, some things Scripture says about Jesus should be understood to refer to His human nature, other things to His divine nature, and still others to both.[17] For example, when Jesus says "I thirst," this does not mean that God thirsts insofar as He is God Himself, but that God thirsts *through* the human nature He has assumed. Strictly speaking, then, the Chalcedonian definition of God is such that He cannot thirst as man can thirst; He cannot be literally *in* a human nature. This theology regards the humanity of Jesus as

---

[17] Augustine, *On the Trinity*, A. Haddan, trans., Book I, ch. 9-13, *Nicene and Post-Nicene Fathers*, Vol. III, P. Schaff, ed., pp. 27-36.

a "veil" which conceals God even as it indirectly reveals Him. To use a modern metaphor, the human Jesus is not "God with us," but a mediator who "points beyond" Himself to God. Or as Augustine stated this same idea: the Word raises us through His humanity to His divinity.[18]

To conceive God to be such that He cannot be present *in* Jesus of Nazareth, but only through Him, is the characteristic of "Hellenism." This Greek attitude assumes that God's divinity is a nature (or essence) which is, in principle, incapable of being in the world. Hence, God must always be "beyond" or "above" or "in the depths" of the world, and He can only manifest Himself through it. Such a scheme makes it impossible to regard the humanity of Jesus as essential to God's own being. This understanding of the humanity of Jesus Christ as nonessential to God is, of course, also consistent with western theology's conviction that the incarnation was not necessary to the fulfillment of God's purpose in creating the world, but a contingency related to Adam's fall and redemption. How far this is from the Sabbath conception of God as one who can enter time and space and sanctify our ordinary lives by His personal presence! The "anthropomorphic" biblical God is not defined in such a way that it is impossible for Him to enter the world. So He enters in.

Today it is *au courant* to call for the "de-Hellenization" of Christianity. But, in fact, the Church began de-Hellenizing Chalcedonian theology in the very moment the Council was disbanded. In fact, only a hundred years later, at the Second Council of Constantinople (553 A.D.), the inadequacies of Chalcedon were fully overcome. However, the western Church has tended to ignore the later ecumenical statements. The extraordinary influence of Augustine's theology in the west fixed its thought in Chalcedonian patterns. For this reason, the western Church has regarded Chalcedon as the terminus and effectual norm of Christological formulation. John Leith exemplifies this western bias when he writes: "While the definition of Chalcedon did not satisfy the Church of the fifth century [i.e., in the time of Chalcedon itself] or the Church since then, its critics have never been able to produce a definition that in the judgment of the Church improves upon Chalcedon."[19] From this statement one would not suspect that a major ecumenical Council of the Church formally

[18] *Ibid.*, Book IV, ch. 18, pp. 81 f.
[19] *Creeds of the Churches*, J. Leith, ed. (New York, 1963), p. 35.

improved upon the definition of Chalcedon in the *very next century*. Nor would one be aware of the fact that Chalcedonian Christology is relatively primitive, confining its attention exclusively to the two natures of Christ and thereby intensifying the neglect of His *person*.

At II Constantinople Hellenism was overthrown and the question left unanswered by Chalcedon was settled: Jesus Christ, the subject of the two natures, is Himself God in person. This means that the human nature no less than the divine nature is part of God's Godhead, manifesting His holiness, and filled with His dignity. The babe born in the stable is the person of God being born. The incarnation is, on this view, essential to the inner life of God himself. God's becoming man is a part of God's very "Godness." This is a very different view from that stated in the formula of Chalcedon. According to Chalcedon, it is part of God's "manness" to be born of Mary, but it is not part of his "Godness" to be born of her. Chalcedon states this matter as follows: that Mary is called *theotokos* ("Mother of God") because she gave birth to the *human nature* that the Son of God assumed. But II Constantinople rejects this view. According to this later council, Mary is *literally theotokos*. She is not called *theotokos* analogically, i. e., because she is the mother of the humanity that the Word assumes. Rather, she is the mother of the Word Himself—since the Word is literally "begotten" of her by the Holy Spirit. To deny this is to imply that Mary is not called *theotokos* in a univocal way, but only "by misuse of language and not truly, or by analogy, believing that only a mere man was born of her, and that God the Word was not incarnate of her, but that the incarnation of God the Word resulted only from the fact that He united Himself to that man who was born [of her]."[20]

The Second Council of Constantinople completely resolves the "in/through" problem we have considered above. To speak about God present only *through* Jesus' humanity is to presuppose that this humanity is not part of Jesus' being God. But according to Constantinople this understanding of the incarnation is wrong. We should not say that Jesus' humanity is His "manness," while His divinity is His "Godness" (as if His "Godness" were manifested "through" His humanness). Rather, we should say that His humanity is His "Godness" in the same way and to the same degree that His divinity is His "Godness" (so that His "Godness" is present "in" His humanness). For the one who is the mother of His humanity is also, and

[20] Art. 6, II Constantinople. *Creeds of the Churches*, p. 48.

literally, the mother of Him as the Word. This is why we see God in Jesus' very humanity, why Jesus' words are God's very words, why Jesus' touch is God's very touch, and why Jesus' birth is the birth of God Himself. Such a view implies the worship of Jesus. But to worship the human Jesus of Nazareth as God is the doctrine of ecumenical Christianity.

The difference between the Christologies of Chalcedon and II Constantinople can be further clarified by stating the conceptual distinction that governs the "in/through" forms of religious speaking. Chalcedonian Christology is *dyadic;* Constantinopolitan Christology is *triadic.* "Dyadic" and "triadic" refer to the number of terms required to explain the name "Jesus Christ." The dyadic formula is: Jesus Christ is "God-man." The triadic formula is: Jesus Christ is "the God who is God-man." The dyadic formula explains Jesus simply in terms of His two natures. The triadic formula explains Jesus not only in terms of His two natures, but also by defining His person: "the God (person) who is God-man (the two natures)." In dyadic Christology, Jesus Christ is the mediator between God in heaven and men on earth. In triadic Christology, Jesus is the God of heaven now present with men on earth. Only a triadic Christology is adequate to the requirement of Sabbath holiness, i. e., to the requirement that God in person be present with us in space and time. To have communion with "the God who is God-man" is, therefore, the chief end of man. God's theocracy requires all life to be ordered to this *telos,* since the world has been made for the manifestation of the glory of God in the person of Jesus Christ. In this way, the ecumenical Christology of Constantinople finds expression in the American vision of space and time sanctified by God's Sabbath presence. "The world," says Edwards, "was made for the Son of God especially."[21] "What He sought as His last end was God's last end in the creation of the world."[22]

THE VIRGIN MOTHER OF GOD

It is still common among western theologians to dismiss the Christology of II Constantinople as monophysite (one-natured, or monadic). This charge can only be excused as failing to understanding both the

21 *An Unpublished Essay of Edwards on the Trinity,* G. Fisher, ed. (New York, 1903), p. 132.
22 Jonathan Edwards, *Dissertation concerning the End for Which God Created the World, The Works of President Edwards* (New York, 1881), Vol. II, p. 225.

conceptual sophistication of this ecumenical Christology and the
critical principle by which this conceptual sophistication is achieved,
viz., the rule of "double-begottenness." According to this rule, the
beginning of the existence of the Word of God is not more properly
asserted of His begottenness of the Father than of His begottenness
of the Virgin Mary. This is the crucial statement from II Constantinople:

If anyone does not confess that God the Word was twice begotten, the
first before all time from the Father, non-temporal and bodiless, the other
in the last days when He came down from the heavens and was incarnate
by the holy, glorious, *theotokos,* ever-virgin Mary, and born of her, let
him be anathema.[23]

Here the "two natures" formula of Chalcedon is succeeded by the
"double-begottenness" formula. The level of the Christological discussion has shifted from *what* Jesus is to *who* Jesus is. It has shifted
from talking about His nature to talking about His person. Being
begotten is proper to persons, not to natures; being begotten refers to
the beginning of existence per se. By binding together the two beginnings of the Son, the formula of II Constantinople explains who
the very *person* begotten of Mary is. The person begotten of Mary
is one and the same as the person begotten of the Father, i. e., Mary is
as properly the mother of the Son of God as the Father is His Father.
Who is Jesus, the Babe of Mary? He is God in person!

There is, of course, no comparable case of a person's having a
"double beginning." Even Plato's preexistent souls did not begin to
exist a second time when they entered into bodies. Moreover, the
Constantinopolitan formula prohibits such analogies since they suggest that Mary is only analogously, and not truly "Mother of God."
The rule of Constantinople in this way excludes all explanations of
the incarnation which might be construed as suggesting that the Son
of God did not truly begin to exist in time. Such apparently orthodox
statements as, "The Word assumed flesh," or "The Son took humanity
up into His person," violate this rule since they suggest that the
person of the Son did not really begin to exist in time. Such statements are accommodations to Hellenistic modes of thinking. The sole
non-Hellenistic explanation of the method of incarnation is the
virgin birth, since this presupposes that from His very conception the

[23] Art. 2, II Constantinople. *Creeds of the Churches,* p. 46.

one in Mary's womb is God. To think, for example, that Joseph begets the child of Mary and that God simply unites Himself to the child thus begotten is to deny that God truly begins to exist in time. From these considerations, we see that there is a necessary reason for the virgin birth. It is implied by the proper understanding of Jesus Christ as God.

The rule of "double-begottenness" is not itself a determinate Christological confession, but a linguistic criterion for excluding improper ways of speaking about Jesus Christ. Just as the rule of the "two natures" is not itself a confession of faith, but a criterion that guides us to the affirmation that "Jesus Christ is God-man," so the rule of "double-begottenness" directs our thinking until we arrive at the sole unambiguously correct confession about Jesus Christ: *theotokos,* "Mary is the Mother of God." Note that *theotokos* is a Christological affirmation. It intends to specify something about God Himself, namely, that He is truly begotten in time.

At the beginning of this section, I indicated that a correct Christological confession affirms unconditionally that Jesus is God in person. But were we to say simply "Jesus Christ is God," this confession might be interpreted in a monophysite (monadic) manner. For such an affirmation does not mention His humanity and makes no distinction between His divine nature and His divine person. Hence, this confession does not exclude Patripassianism, the supposition that the Father Himself suffered on the cross. For this reason, I believe we should affirm that Jesus Christ is God in person by means of the *theotokos,* the confession that "Mary is the Mother of God."

Protestants and Catholics seem to be about equally removed from affirming this true ecumenical Christology. The Catholic Church affirms the *theotokos,* but neglects the rule of double-begottenness. That is, it tends to stress the Chalcedonian perspective: that Mary is mother of the *humanity* of the God-man, that (since the humanity she provides is for the sake of redemption) Mary is coredemptrix, that there is a special holiness in her person—especially in her state of virginity.[24] By focusing on the Chalcedonian perspective, Catholic theology neglects the rule of double-begottenness. This means that it

---

[24] Cyril Vollert, *A Theology of Mary* (New York, 1965) is a clear example of "Chalcedonian Mariology." It focuses relentlessly on her motherhood of the *humanity* of Jesus Christ rather than on her motherhood of the divine person. The title "Mother of the Church" becomes, therefore, more appropriate to her than even the title "Mother of God"—since she originates redeemed humanity.

fails to see why the virgin birth is necessarily implied by the mere fact of incarnation, i. e., implied as an "analytic truth." Rather, Catholic theology supposes that the doctrine of the virgin birth is a synthetic truth, reporting an additional extra-Christological grace that is given through the person of Mary. Hence, the Catholic Church understands the *theotokos* to be a Mariological rather than a Christological confession.

From the argument I have developed, however, we must conclude that the deficiency of Catholic Mariology is not that it is too developed, but that it is not developed enough. If Catholic Mariology were fully developed as an integral part of Christology, there would be no tendency to exalt Mary's human nature and her virginity per se. Moreover, we could then even account for the special status of Mary in the Christian faith: for God would have dignified her by His presence *in* her womb. She would be the first to be "indwelt" by God, the first to be personally holy through *union* with a Holy Person. But such a personal holiness does not result from the holiness of the creature himself; rather, it results from God's own personal presence *in* (not *with*) him. There are, of course, certain moral prerequisites for receiving such a dignity; but these moral prerequisites cannot be the basis for making Mary the object of her own separate cult.

On the other hand, in spite of its culpable neglect of the *theotokos,* Protestant theology has often been faithful to the rule of double begottenness. This is to be explained not as the result of Protestant attention to the ecumenical creeds, but because of the pietistic emphasis upon the necessity for a vivid personal experience of the incarnate Jesus Christ as God. I have already presented examples of this pietistic emphasis as it was mediated through Edwards. It is, however, important to stress that the similar vision of John Wesley was no less important in shaping the Christology of modern Protestantism—especially in America. As Wesley noted, to stress that the incarnate Jesus is unconditionally *God* was an innovation in western Christianity. In his journal, he wrote: "About noon I preached at Warrington; I am afraid, not to the taste of some of my hearers, as my subject led me to speak strongly and explicitly on the Godhead of Christ. But that I cannot help, for on this I *must* insist as the foundation of all our hope."[25]

[25] *Journal,* "Tues. 5 April, 1768" (V, 253-54). Cited in R. Burtner and R. Chiles, eds., *A Compend of Wesley's Theology* (Nashville, Tenn., 1954), p. 76.

The pietistic-revivalistic-Wesleyan sense of Jesus as God is a practical acquiescence in the rule of double-begottenness. This same religious consciousness was the hidden passion behind Protestant biblical study in the nineteenth century, and, in the twentieth century, Karl Barth has written an entire dogmatics which is, in effect, controlled by the Constantinopolitan rule. No western theologian has ever surpassed Barth in binding together "the two beginnings of the Son." Most recently, this Protestant religious consciousness has been given summary dogmatic expression in the original basis of the World Council of Churches: "Jesus Christ is God and Savior." This unconditional affirmation that the person of Jesus is God, an affirmation that goes beyond the traditional God-man formula, is the Protestant development that parallels certain recent tendencies in Catholic theology to interpret Marian doctrine Christologically and thus move western Christianity "beyond Chalcedon."

To summarize: my argument thus far is that the question *cur deus homo* should be subordinated to the question *cur creatio*. When this is done, Christology will be determined by the requirements of the Sabbath. The Sabbath guest must be God in person present with us. To think of Jesus Christ in this way requires us to shift the scope of Christology from redemption to sanctification and to develop the form of Christology to stress that Jesus is God in person. These changes do not undermine, but undergird the Chalcedonian affirmations. Only if man is created for the dignity of holines is redemption truly important. Only if Jesus Christ is truly God born of the Virgin can our lives be dignified by the presence of the Holy One in time and space. The Sabbath is not only made for Jesus Christ; it also prescribes a right understanding of him. From this right understanding of Jesus Christ, we also see why Mary is *theotokos*. The *theotokos* is not presently a major element in American religion, but it is implied by the doctrines already affirmed by it. In explicating these implications, I am attempting to fill a certain *lacuna* in American religion and complete my doctrinal system.

"ONE PERSON IN TWO PERSONS"

Although the world is made for Jesus Christ, it is not made only for Him. The incarnation fulfills the Sabbath intention of God for His creation, but this is not its sole fulfillment. For God manifests His holiness in the world not in one way, but in two. The world is sanctified not only by God's presence "with us," but also by His presence "in us." This second form of God's presence is by the indwelling of the Holy Spirit. In fact, by the Holy Spirit's dwelling "in us" we are personally sanctified, for this is not simply a *communion* with God, but a real *union*.

In the communion of "God with us" there is a relation between two or more persons, only one of whom is actually holy. Therefore, when we say that the world is "sanctified" by the incarnation, we understand this sanctification analogically, i. e., we ascribe the dignity of holiness to the world because the Holy One is with us—not because the world itself is holy. But, when God sanctifies the world by His presence "in us," then we mean that the world itself is holy, a manifestation of the very glory of God Himself. In this sense, holiness is ascribed to the world univocally and not just analogically. This actual hallowing of mankind in its spatio-temporal existence is what God seeks as His second end for the creation. Hence, the world is made not only for Jesus Christ, but also for the Holy Spirit.

It may seem that the argument I have developed in this chapter excludes the possibility of any personal sanctification of men, for would this not mean that holiness is *communicated* to the creature? Or would it mean, alternatively, that men cease to be creatures— being transubstantiated into a part of God Himself? But, in fact, neither of these consequences follows if we properly understand the manner of the Spirit's indwelling. For the Spirit is "in us" in such a way that holiness still remains the incommunicable dignity of God alone.

Our reflection on the Holy Spirit must follow the same method as that employed in our analysis of Christology. That is, just as we asked *cur deus homo,* so we should also seek to discover what reasons there are for thinking that God is a Holy Spirit and indwells His creation. Just as we saw that the incarnation was required to fulfill God's purpose in creating the world, so we shall see that the Holy Spirit also fulfills God's purpose. The incarnation took place in order to fulfill what the Sabbath requires; but the indwelling of the Spirit takes place to fulfill the requirements of both the Sabbath and the incarnation. For both the Sabbath and the incarnation anticipate the coming of the Spirit, and each for its own special reason. The immediate, though subordinate, reason for Christ's sending the Spirit is *moral,* i. e., to fulfill what faith, hope, and love require. The remote or indirect, though chief, reason for Christ's sending the Spirit is *religious,* i. e., to manifest God's holiness. We can schematize these two reasons as follows:

a. Sabbath requires incarnation;

b. incarnation requires Spirit (moral reason);

c. therefore, Sabbath requires Spirit (religious reason).

In this section, I shall discuss the moral reason for the sending of the Holy Spirit, taking up the religious reason in the following one. In conjunction with this first problem, I shall suggest how the indwelling of the Spirit itself should be understood (how the Spirit is "in us"); in conjunction with the second problem, I shall explain why Christians should affirm that the "Holy Spirit" is not just a metaphor symbolizing God's activity or power, but is the name of a distinct person of God.

The Moral Reason for the Holy Spirit. The coming of Jesus Christ into the world aims at sanctification. Being born of a woman, God is with us as a friend, i. e., He is present to us in the most intimate way that one man can be united with another. In fact, there is no closer or more perfect form of presence among created beings than the friendship that unites two persons with one another in faith, hope, and love. Gabriel Marcel's analysis of these affections reveals a profound sensitivity to the character of intersubjective presence. Protestant theological reflection on the power of religious language to commit, renew, and forgive reveals the same appreciation of the unconditionedness characteristic of personal communion. In this type of moral union (communion, friendship, "being-withness") a man is united with his fellow man almost as closely as he is one with himself.

When God enters into our lives in Jesus Christ, He determines to be morally present to us. That is, He determines to be present to us not only as God in person, but also as one who shares our human nature, seeking and accepting the unconditional obligations implicit in such a moral union. It should be noted, however, that we have not yet discovered any nonsoteriological ("nonredemptive") reason why God should seek to be present with us in this way. The Sabbath requires only that God be personally present in the world, not that He be present by means of incarnation. God's personal presence and His presence by incarnation can be distinguished from one another. The personal presence of God in time and space does not require, as a condition of its occurrence, that God become man. For example, God is personally present to the oxen on the Sabbath and yet He does not assume the nature of an ox. And God is personally present with Israel in the Temple, but He is not present as one born of a woman. So it seems that God might have manifested His holiness in the world without becoming man. And I suspect that this is precisely the point that Judaism would emphasize: the Sabbath requires a Sabbath guest, but not an incarnation.

Later, I shall argue that there is a reason why the Sabbath guest must be present in the world by means of incarnation, but for the moment I grant that this does not seem necessary. There seems to be no reason why God's chief purpose in creating the world could not have been fulfilled without His placing Himself under new obligations to man by Himself becoming man. For this is exactly what the incarnation implies: by becoming incarnate God accepts these new moral obligations toward man that are appropriate to friendship among men. If God had not become man, He would have been under no moral obligation to suffer for men and to preserve them from death. But, by becoming man and a friend to man, God owes man whatever friendship among men requires. This is the "new obligation" that God assumes by becoming incarnate, and this is why classical theology has rightly insisted that the surety of our redemption is the true humanity of Jesus Christ.

Since it is unusual to argue that the incarnation places God under new obligations toward man, let me suggest a parallel: the case of marriage. A marriage creates new moral obligations for the covenanting parties. Only those who have pledged their troth to one another are under an unconditional obligation to love, honor, and cleave only to each other for better, for worse, for richer, for poorer, in sickness, and in health. Becoming one flesh creates new moral obligations for man just as being born in the flesh creates new moral obligations for God. Only those who have pledged themselves to one another in marriage are under an unconditional obligation to endure all suffering with one another. Hence, just as marriage is the presupposition of the lifelong responsibility of two specific persons for one another, so the incarnation is the presupposition of God's lifelong responsibility for man, even unto His death on the cross. God died for us because He accepted the moral requirements of friendship with us. And we shall see that this is also the reason that He sends us the Holy Spirit.

Friendship requires a certain equality of the parties involved, and it is this "equality" that God accepts in His becoming man. A perfect communion, or friendship, is unconditional; it ought never to be broken. A mutual commitment of faith, hope, and love makes two persons one in understanding and affection. This unity requires them to do things for one another that exceed all that is implied in the fact of their mere individuality. For example, perfect friendship so unites persons in love that either would lay down his life for the other even though the fact of their separate individualities might be construed as forbidding such an act. Yet because of their moral union (i. e., "communion"), two persons will affirm that they ought to act as if they were one person even though they are not one person. The love that they have for each other seems to create an ought, or a requiredness, that exceeds everything involved in their separate individualities. Love makes two persons "one in relation" even though they are "two in individuality." For this reason, two persons who love one another unconditionally do not regard their separate individualities as excusing unconditional responsibility for one another. In fact, because they love one another, they feel they *ought* to do things that are made impossible by the fact of their individuality. Love tries to do even what it cannot do. So, even when we cannot suffer as our friend himself suffers, we still suffer sympathetically, or "with him." Even when we cannot die for our friends, we still seek to die with them—as if undergoing in our own being what is undergone in the being of another. In this way, communion affirms the rightness of things that individuality seems to make impossible: namely, that the love of two should not be destroyed by the death of either one.[26]

The Christian Church has always recognized that Christ's love for us, attested by His dying on our behalf, makes it morally right that our communion with Him should never be broken. Moreover, theology has sometimes singled out his rightness itself as the basis for our hope in eternal life. But although communion with Christ is the necessary condition of eternal life, it is not its sufficient condition. What is morally right is not, for this reason alone, actually going to occur. This is why even our personal communion with God Himself does not, per se, give us sufficient grounds for affirming that we shall not

[26] The argument here presupposes my previous analysis of three kinds of unity. Because relations ("communion") are no less real than individuals, what is required because of relation is no less than what is required because of individuality.

die. No theologian has ever distinguished these two aspects of the problem with greater acumen than St. Augustine in his *Soliloquies*. In this treatise, Augustine shows that the moral and rational fitness of the soul for eternal communion with God is not a sufficient ground for asserting that the soul will actually have eternal life. An "ought" by itself does not create an "is." What ought to occur can only occur if something is done to make it occur. This is why the love of Christ for us is not a sufficient basis for affirming we shall actually attain eternal life; the only sufficient basis for such a hope is what Jesus Christ does because He loves us.

Because of His love, Jesus Christ sends the Holy Spirit to preserve us from death. Thereby He accomplishes what His moral union with us requires. In fact, sending the Holy Spirit is the chief thing that Jesus seeks by His ministry of obedience to God. For the purpose of Jesus' ministry is to fulfill all that love and righteousness require. But what they chiefly require—given the fact of the incarnation—is that our personal communion with Him not be broken by death. The incarnation creates a new moral requirement and the chief purpose of Jesus' ministry is to fulfill this requirement. Hence, the aim of His ministry is to send the Holy Spirit to dwell in our hearts and thereby fulfill what love requires: that nothing separate us from the love of Christ. Hence, just as the incarnation effects what the Sabbath requires, so the indwelling of the Holy Spirit effects what the incarnation requires.

The creeds of the Church name the Holy Spirit as the person of God whom Jesus sends to bestow eternal life upon us. The Holy Spirit is author of "the Holy, Catholic Church, the communion of saints, the forgiveness of sins, the resurrection of the body, and the life everlasting." Jesus does not bestow these gifts directly; rather, He bestows them through the Spirit whom He sends. The Holy Spirit gives us eternal life by uniting Himself to us in a unique way. His indwelling is a form of presence which is closer and more "unitive" than even the most perfect communion among created beings. Indwelling is a divine, or uncreated, form of presence. It is the very perichoresis that unites the persons of God with each other. Hence, when the Holy Spirit indwells us, we are lifted into the very life of God Himself.

Creatures cannot indwell one another. Rather, the perfect form of unity among creatures is the moral communion of friendship. When Jesus Christ sends the Holy Spirit to dwell in us, however, He makes

God present to us in a way which exceeds even the most perfect moral communion. In our union with the Holy Spirit, we are joined to Him even more closely than we are joined to ourselves (since even "self-consciousness" is a form of created presence). Hence, Scripture tells us that the Spirit knows us not only better than even our closest friends know us, but even better than we know ourselves. For when we do not know our true desires, the Holy Spirit interprets them to God for us. When we do not know the way to turn, the Spirit leads us. When we are weighed down by doubts and despair, the Spirit preserves our soul. When we cannot hold our lives in our own hands, then we know they will be held in the hand of God. The man in whom the Spirit dwells, dwells in the Spirit, the Comforter whom our friend Jesus Christ sends us.

The Church has not yet formulated a dogmatic explanation of the indwelling of the Holy Spirit in a human person. She has defined the relation of God to creation as *ex nihilo;* she has defined the presence of God in Jesus Christ as "one person in two natures"; but she has never defined the union of the Holy Spirit with the soul, or very person, of a man. I suggest, however, that Scripture and ecumenical dogma require the minimum affirmation that the Holy Spirit indwells a man as "one person in two persons." This formula is to be explained as follows: when the Holy Spirit indwells a created person, He does not assume a human nature. Rather, He unites Himself with a created person or individual existence in an "uncreated" way. In this indwelling the distinctive individualities of both the human person and the Holy Spirit are maintained, and yet they are spoken of as a single subject. They "indwell" one another. In this way, the act of either is referred to the other: "I pray, yet not I, but the Spirit in me . . .," says the Apostle. "Hear the Word of the Lord . . .," says the prophet, speaking with a human voice.

On the other hand, the indwelling Spirit not only unites Himself with a human person, but He also indwells and is united with Jesus Christ, whose Spirit He is. In this way, the Spirit is one person in two persons: He is in Jesus Christ and He is in the created person whom He indwells. He is a common subject of two other distinct subjects. There is, therefore, a certain parallel to the incarnation here. Just as Jesus Christ is an uncreated person who unites in Himself both divine and human natures, so the Holy Spirit is an uncreated person who unites in Himself both another divine person and a human person.

L

Just as Jesus Christ assumes human nature into Himself, so the Holy Spirit takes a human person into Himself—although there is no *hypostatic union* of the Holy Spirit with the human person. The union of the Holy Spirit with the human person is not hypostatic because the Spirit is united with a man in the same way that He is united with Jesus Christ, i. e., by mutual indwelling or perichoresis. This is a real, though not a hypostatic, union—for in the perichoresis of the Spirit with the soul of man the two persons remain distinct. (Such a conclusion is implied by the formula "one person in two persons.") From these reflections we see that the indwelling of the Spirit in man not only resembles the mutual indwelling of the persons of the Trinity, but even extends their perichoresis into the creation. In this way, men enter into the very life of God.[27]

By affirming that the indwelling Holy Spirit is "one person in two persons," we also make it clear that the Spirit intends to establish our eternal communion with Jesus Christ. That is, He intends to sustain the Church and the communion of saints (and whatever is necessarily implied thereby). Were we, for example, to assert that the Holy Spirit indwells man alone (i. e., "one person in one person"), this might be interpreted to mean that the Spirit thereby intends to make men "Christs" or that He even makes men more than Christ by creating a "third stage" of history. But the formula "one person in two persons" excludes such interpretations by stating that the Holy Spirit indwells a man by sustaining that man in an eternal communion with Christ. The coming of the Spirit thereby confirms the finality of the incarnation. Our assumption into the life of God through the indwelling Holy Spirit is for the sake of making real that which the incarnation and the crucifixion have made right: namely, that nothing shall ever separate us from the love of Christ.

We must now recall our earlier warning that the formula "one person in two persons" is *minimum*. In fact, the Holy Spirit is one person in many persons. He is the divine subject uniting Jesus Christ and His Church. He is God as the subject of community. Moreover, the Holy Spirit not only unites men mystically with Christ, but He also unites them mystically with each other. Thereby we are brought into the communion of saints, into a living communion with those who have

[27] There are striking resemblances between my proposals respecting the Holy Spirit and those of Heribert Mühlen, *Der Heilige Geist als Person* (Münster, 1963). He too suggests the "one person in two persons" formula, though he seems to interpret this in a rather more Augustinian manner than I.

passed from this earth and are now alive in Christ. By the indwelling of the Holy Spirit we are not only never separated from the love of Christ, but are also never separated from those we love. For this reason we may say that the Holy Spirit not only *indwells,* but, more precisely, *"interdwells* my brother and myself for our communion with God and with one another in Christ Jesus."[28]

WHY THE HOLY SPIRIT IS GOD IN PERSON

Western theology has not ascribed to the Holy Spirit a function sufficient to justify our calling Him God in person. It has attempted to ascribe such a divine function to the work of Christ. But its energies have been exhausted on this problem, and it has handled the parallel question with respect to the Holy Spirit not by argument, but by analogy, viz., that the relation between God and the Spirit should be "understood" to resemble the relation between God and Jesus Christ. All historians of theology know the paucity of discussions concerning the Spirit—and the embarrassment characteristic of even these few. And all Christians know that the Church has never offered an explanation of the Spirit's union with a human person comparable to the "one person, two natures" formula. Moreover, there is even a marked tendency among many western Christians to deny altogether that the Spirit is a person in the same sense that the Father and the Son are persons. For Augustine, the Spirit is the relation between the Father and the Son; for contemporary Barthians (e. g. Berkhof), the Spirit is not a personal name at all, but a name signifying the power of Jesus Christ.[29] Throughout western Christianity it has become common to define the Spirit in impersonal ways: He is a power, an energy, an activity, a bond, a relation ("love"), and so forth.

One of the acknowledged peculiarities of American Christianity is its opposition to this general western tendency. For in its preoccupation with holiness, American Christianity is seeking to ascribe to the Holy Spirit a work sufficient to justify calling Him God in person.

[28] Joseph Haroutunian, *God With Us* (Philadelphia, 1965), p. 77.

[29] "Christ as Spirit permeates and sanctifies the created world, until all things are summed up under Christ as their Head and mankind is recreated according to his image. . . . The Spirit is Person because he is God acting as a Person. However, we cannot say that the Spirit is a Person distinct from God the Father. He is a Person in relation to us, not in relation to God; for he is the personal God himself in relation to us." Hendrikus Berkhof, *The Doctrine of the Holy Spirit* (Richmond, 1964), p. 116.

This preoccupation is manifested institutionally in Pentecostalism and the modern holiness sects—which were cradled in America. And these movements represent a third form of western Christianity no less unique and important than either Reformation Protestantism or Roman Catholicism. Historians who fail to view this development within the full history of the Church and its theology do not sense the significance of what is happening. William McLoughlin, for example, lumps the Pentecostalists with the fundamentalists and argues that they are no such "third force."[30] But this is not the case. The holiness movement is an institutional evidence that a major theological reorientation has taken place in American Christianity—a reorientation which pervades the life and thought of even the more traditional Churches.

I might elaborate this point by gathering a wide range of evidences. But perhaps it is more important to emphasize that those theologians who shaped the American understanding of Christianity were themselves aware that they were breaking with the dominant western tradition. John Wesley, for example, believed his doctrine of "Christian perfection" was a biblical teaching neglected by the western Church. He conceived this perfection to be the holiness in a believer resulting from the indwelling Spirit. (Actually, Wesley's doctrine probably stems in large part from his reading of the early Eastern Orthodox mystics—another indication of the similarities between American religion and Orthodoxy.[31]) And America's greatest theologian, the supposedly traditional Calvinist Jonathan Edwards, specifically argued that western theology had never ascribed to the Holy Spirit a work sufficient to justify calling Him God. In his very first published writing, Edwards set out to correct this deficiency.[32]

[30] William McLoughlin, "Is There a Third Force in Christendom," *Daedalus*, 96/1, p. 51.

[31] "In the thought and piety of the early Church [Wesley] discovered what he thereafter regarded as the normative pattern of catholic Christianity. He was particularly interested in 'Marcarius the Egyptian' and Ephraim Syrus." *John Wesley*, A. Outler, ed. (New York, 1964), p. 9 f.

[32] "If we suppose no more than used to be supposed about the Holy Ghost, the honour of the Holy Ghost is not equal in any sense to the Father and the Son's; nor is there an equal part of the glory of this work belonging to Him. Merely to apply to us, or immediately to give or to hand to us blessing purchased, after it is purchased, is subordinate to the other two persons." "Treatise on Grace," *Selections from the Unpublished Writings of Jonathan Edwards*, A. Grosart, ed. (Edinburgh, 1865), p. 51. In his earliest writing, *God Glorified in Man's Dependence*, Edwards makes an explicit effort to overcome this subordination.

Strictly speaking, except for Orthodoxy, the only genuine Christian trinitarianism has been found in American religion. Western theology, in spite of its formal confession that God is triune, is functionally and theoretically binitarian. Functionally, it is concerned with the Father and the Son, creation and redemption. Theoretically, it has developed the *filioque* doctrine, which "upgrades" Christ by "downgrading" the Holy Spirit. It has remained for American Christianity to recover authentic trinitarian doctrine as an expression of its theocratic faith. H. Richard Niebuhr notes the threefold focus of this theocratic faith, remarking that

the Christian movement in America began with a confession of loyalty to the sovereign God and moved on to experience the reality of the reign of Christ. From the experience it went on to the prayer, "Thy kingdom come; thy will be done on earth as it is in heaven." The three notes of faith in the sovereignty, the experience of the love of Christ and hope of ultimate redemption are inseparable. . . . The theological definition of the relation of these three elements is as difficult as the definition of the Trinity.[33]

We have already seen that this new perspective has led American Christians to understand God the Creator and Jesus Christ in new ways. I shall now take up the third person of the Trinity, the one with whom American Christianity has been uniquely preoccupied. Can we understand the Spirit's work as sufficient to justify confessing Him to be God in person? In what follows, I shall continue my constructive theological presentation and show that the arguments I have already developed will allow us to answer this question affirmatively.

The Religious Reason for the Holy Spirit. The moral reason for Christ's sending the Holy Spirit is not sufficient to justify our calling the Holy Spirit "God in person." This is the case because only He who does the distinguishing work of God is properly called God. But to maintain our moral communion with Christ is not such a work, since it is not the reason for which God created the world. We can see this by considering the following: (a) God's purpose in creating the world is the Sabbath, i. e., He creates the world in order to manifest His holiness in space and time. (b) This sanctification requires God's personal presence in the world. (c) But this personal presence of God in space and time does not seem to require that He be present by

[33] H. Richard Niebuhr, *The Kingdom of God in America* (New York, 1959), pp. 127 f.

means of incarnation. For God could be personally present with Israel in the Temple even though He was not incarnate, and God can be personally present to oxen on the Sabbath even though He has not assumed the form of an ox. (d) Therefore, God's presence by means of incarnation seems to have some other reason than that which accounts for His mere personal entrance into space and time. (e) If it has some other reason, then God did not become incarnate in order to fulfill His original purpose in the creation of the world. (Usually this other reason is understood to be soteriological, i. e., God became incarnate for the sake of man's redemption.) (f) Since the sending of the Holy Spirit is required because of Christ's humanity and His moral union with us (and not because of Jesus Christ's personal presence qua Holy One), the indwelling Spirit does not seem to be intended by God as part of His original purpose for creation. The Spirit seems to be simply for the sake of man's redemption. (g) Therefore, the indwelling of the Spirit is not a work sufficient to justify calling Him "God in person," since His indwelling does not have the same scope as the work of creation itself.

The only way to avoid the final conclusion in this argument is to discover a nonsoteriological reason for the incarnation. For if God became man solely for the sake of our redemption, then whatever is consequent upon His incarnation alone must have redemption as its scope. That is, it must be bound up with God's purpose for the sixth day (the creation and restoration of man in the *imago dei*) rather than with God's purpose for the Sabbath Day (the sanctification of the world). Only if the reason for God's taking *flesh* is more than soteriological will the purpose of the Spirit's indwelling be more than soteriological. If the primary work of the Holy Spirit is to be sanctification, then Jesus Christ must have become true man not simply for the sake of our redemption, but also for the sake of the sanctification of the world. However, since His human nature is not itself a "personal presence of God," His incarnation per se cannot be understood to be a work of sanctification. In what other sense, then, may we understand God's humanity to be for the sake of sanctification, i. e., for the sake of fulfilling God's Sabbath purpose?

God's becoming personally present in the world by means of incarnation requires Him also to send the Holy Spirit. We have seen that there is a moral reason why Christ sends the Holy Spirit to us, but we have not found any reason why God should place

Himself under this moral requirement. Why did God become man and thereby accept the moral obligation to send His Holy Spirit to dwell in our hearts? If we could only discover a nonsoteriological reason for God's becoming man, this would be a second answer to the question *cur spiritus sanctus*. Moreover, this second answer would be more fundamental than the first—for the moral reason for the Holy Spirit presupposes that Jesus Christ is truly human, and hence presupposes some reason why He became human. Therefore, to explain why God became incarnate (i. e., became present in *flesh*) is to give the chief, or religious, explanation for the indwelling of the Holy Spirit in the world.

If we refer our question about God's true humanity back to His Sabbath purpose, we shall discover the nonsoteriological reason for the incarnation. God became personally present *with us* for the sake of sanctification and He became personally present *with us in the flesh* for the same reason, i. e., for the sake of manifesting His glory, or making Himself personally present in the world. Hence God became man for the same reason that He created the world. But, whereas God created the Sabbath Day for the sake of manifesting the holiness of the Son, God became incarnate for the sake of manifesting the holiness of the Spirit. The Sabbath Day requires that God be personally present with us, while the incarnation requires that God be personally present in us. This is why God puts Himself under the moral obligation to send us the Spirit: it is for His own glory, for the presence of His holiness in the world. Moreover, since the indwelling Spirit brings us into the life of God Himself, we may say that God's purpose in creation is to manifest His triune holiness to Himself by making a world and bringing it into His own holy life.

From these considerations we see that the incarnation (or true humanity of Jesus Christ) is not primarily for the sake of our redemption, but for the sake of God's own glory, the sanctification of the world. For God becomes incarnate for the sake of sending the Holy Spirit. The Spirit indwells us, moreover, not chiefly for the sake of our communion with Christ (the moral reason), but for the Spirit's own sake. Just as the chief reason for the presence of God with us is not what He can do for us, but for its own sake, so the chief reason for the presence of God in us is not what He can do for us, but for its own sake. The personal presence of the Holy One is not for the sake of something else; rather, everything else is for its sake. Since the enjoyment of God is the chief end of man, the enjoyment of the Spirit present in us is its own sufficient reason. The moral work of the Holy Spirit is to maintain our communion with Christ, but the "religious" work of the Spirit is simply to be the Holy One dwelling in us. This religious reason fulfills the chief end of God in creating the world, viz., to sanctify all things by His personal presence.

Even though holiness belongs incommunicably to God, the indwelling Holy Spirit personally sanctifies the creature in whom He dwells. That is, on the basis of His indwelling it is proper to say that a man becomes truly holy. We can see why this is the case by recurring to the formula for indwelling: one person in two persons. With this formula in mind, we may argue: (a) If we are to ascribe holiness to a man, we must ascribe it to his person—for holiness is a dignity appropriate to persons and not to natures. (b) By virtue of the Spirit's indwelling, there is a real union between the person of a man and the person of the Holy Spirit. (c) Therefore, with respect to this real union, we may ascribe the holiness proper to the Spirit to the created person in whom He dwells. However, we ascribe this holiness to the creature strictly with respect to the mutual indwelling of his soul with the Spirit. With respect to this perichoresis, a man is personally holy though not "intrinsically" holy. That is, he is not holy either from himself or through himself. Rather, he is holy because the Holy One dwells in him.

Because the santification of man results from a union of persons, man's nature is neither divinized nor transformed by it. The man in whom the Spirit dwells remains fully man. He is not separated out from the rest of humanity. He is not given a "godlike nature." The Spirit creates no "higher life with better faculties," no special visions or charisma, no "extramental" or "extramoral" consciousness.[34] The indwelling Spirit does not aim "to split humanity into two camps" —as Teilhard de Chardin suggests when he writes: "On this side are those, who consider the world that has to be built as a comfortable place to live in. On the other side, there are the others who can only visualize the world as a machine of progress or, better yet, as an organism in a state of progress."[35] The Spirit does not divide mankind into *homo sapiens,* from whom we descend, and *homo progressivus,* "a

[34] The view of Sri Aurobindo as cited by Ernst Benz, *Evolution and Christian Hope* (New York, 1966), p. 205.
[35] Cited *ibid.,* p. 236.

man for whom the future of this earth counts more than its present."[36]

We have already discussed the error of those modern theologies of history which regard holiness as a communicable attribute of God, something that God infuses into the nature of men, transforming them into "men of the future." This kind of spiritual racism—with all its demonic overtones of a superman who is not bound by obligations toward ordinary humanity—has nothing whatsoever to do with the Christian doctrine of the Holy Spirit. However, because of the increasing danger to the world of such heretical doctrines, the Church should now undertake what it has so long neglected, namely, to provide an account of the Spirit's indwelling. The formula "one person in two persons" would seem to provide a minimum justification for those affirmations which are essential to Christian faith while also excluding such ominous modern misunderstandings of the Spirit as the ideology of a "third age" and the spiritual racism of *homo progressivus*.

Finally, the analysis I have presented in this chapter helps us to understand why the Holy Spirit must be God in person. Since His presence sanctifies us, He must be a holy person—for holiness is the incommunicable dignity of the persons of God. By making the world holy, the Spirit fulfills God's chief and ultimate purpose for His creation. *Cur creatio?* For the sake of the indwelling Spirit, for the sake of the sanctification of all things, for the sake of holiness—the glory of God.

Since the Spirit finally accomplishes that for which the world was created, the Spirit is God in person. Since the Spirit fulfills the Sabbath, the Holy Spirit is the Spirit of Sabbath holiness. When Jesus Christ sends Him into the world, the "eternal Sabbath" begins to overflow the confines of the seventh day and to fill all the time and space of history. This, I suggest, is the meaning of the Christian observance of Sunday as a holy day. It is our testimony to the Sabbath, not our repudiation of it. It is a sign that the holiness of the seventh day has begun to "overflow" and fill the other days. In eternity, every day will be the Sabbath Day. The Christian Sunday, therefore, is the extension of the Sabbath presence of God into a new time. It is a sign that the kingdom of God is being established on earth. It is a sign that the eschaton has begun.

Our reflections upon the Holy Spirit have led us to understand why

[36] *Ibid.*, p. 237.

we should confess that the Holy Spirit is God in person. These reflections presuppose that holiness is an incommunicable dignity of God and that the chief purpose of indwelling is sanctification. If we reject these presuppositions, then we shall fall back into the binitarianism of traditional western Christianity and have no sure basis for affirming that the Holy Spirit is God in person. For if the Spirit's sole work were to effect our eternal communion with Christ, to grant us eternal life, to forgive our sins, and to form the Church, then the Spirit might be conceived to be merely an attribute or a power of God. He might be conceived to be merely a "figure of speech" expressing either divine sovereignty or the power of Christ. In fact, to the extent that Scripture speaks about the Holy Spirit apart from His sanctifying work, it does frequently describe Him in impersonal terms: as an energy, a wind, a hand, an effective means. In these contexts, the Spirit either has or expresses the divine nature or power; but He is not unequivocally confessed to be God in person.

The situation I am describing also has parallels in Christology where, as we have seen, by focusing on Christ's redemptive work the Church failed to make an unconditional affirmation that Jesus is God in person. As long as Jesus was affirmed to be merely the mediator between God and man, it was necessary for Him to possess the divine nature and power, but there was no intrinsic necessity for him to be a person of God. Only when Christology is developed in relation to its chief end, viz., sanctification, does the reason for confessing Jesus to be God in person finally appear. In the same way, as long as the Spirit's chief work is not brought into view, He may be called the power of God but He will never be affirmed to be God in person. For such an affirmation is made only with respect to the requirements of sanctification. By bringing this end in view, we see why the Holy Spirit must be a person (since holiness is a dignity appropriate to persons alone) and must also be a person of God (since holiness is a dignity belonging to God alone).

SANCTIFICATION AND THE *FELIX CULPA*

In this chapter I hope to have demonstrated that many of the unique elements of American Christianity can be integrated within a single system. I have acknowledged that the theology developed in this chapter is my own construction. But I believe there are two reasons why it can properly be called American. First, its primary themes are unique to, or persistently characteristic of, American religious history. For where else has the Sabbath been a major doctrinal theme? Where else has intramundane holiness and the personhood of the Holy Spirit been a matter of self-conscious theological reflection? Where else has Jesus been so consistently regarded as the final object of religious faith? And, most decisively, at what other point in Christian history have the Old and New Testaments been regarded as mutually *supplementary*? For it should be noted that the hermeneutical assumption of much American Christianity is that the Old Testament contains content that supplements all that we know from Christ and the Apostles. Hence the Sabbath. Hence the law and the covenant. Hence the theme of theocracy and the glory of God.

There is also a second reason why this theology may be called American. For not only its interpretation of particular doctrines, but even the unique perspective which governs their systematic arrangement is suggested by American religious experience. This systematic arrangement arises naturally when the question of Sabbath holiness, the *cur creatio,* is substituted for the traditional *cur deus homo.* Moreover, it should be noted that the question *cur creatio* not only forms the American theological perspective, but also informs the American attitude toward the world. For it implies that nature is not the norm of human life, but is something made to be shaped to a higher destiny. This understanding of nature undergirds the positive American attitude toward technology, the instrument whereby man transforms his world.

In my argument I have tried to give a theological justification for something that many commentators on American Christianity have described, viz., that its primary concern is sanctification. Man's sin and redemption are essential, but secondary, concerns. At the beginning of this essay, I noted that once the character of American theology had been clearly defined, it then would be possible to raise the question of its truth over against the traditional western theologies of redemption. And it is with this question that I shall conclude.

The argument for the truth of a theology of sanctification is that only in this way can the scriptural doctrine of *redemption* be properly developed, for the doctrine of sanctification undergirds the doctrine of redemption. A theology which makes redemption into its sole or primary theme will be ambivalent about the fact of redemption itself. It will have a "vested interest" in man's sin and weakness, for if these were ever fully overcome, the presupposition of Christ's redeeming work would be lost. Hence, theologies of redemption tenaciously defend the sinfulness of man and view with suspicion every secular therapy that attempts to overcome or alleviate man's weakness. They are politically and socially conservative, threatened by the development of psychoanalysis, social work, and political programs for the improvement of human life. These therapies appear to make religion useless. They cause a loss of vocational purpose in many clergymen, who ask what they can do that the new scientific techniques cannot do better. This is what the secular theologians mean when they say that science and technology are pushing God out of the world: that secular therapies are destroying the anthropological presupposition of a religion whose conception of God is exclusively redemptive.

The modern theologian who has best described the ambivalence of an exclusively redemptive religion with respect to redemption itself is Dietrich Bonhoeffer in his *Letters and Papers from Prison*. He saw that a religion which presupposes the weakness of man will be unable to speak to a self-sufficient "man come of age." Moreover, Bonhoeffer also came to see that for a man to wait upon a religious therapy when a secular therapy is available for his use is for him to avoid accepting responsibility for his destiny. In these emphases, of course, he was echoing the insights of Nietzsche, who called the Christian gospel of redemption a religion for slaves, a religion that denigrates all that appears good in human life in order to magnify the grace of God.

The whole point of my argument in this chapter, however, is to show that redemption is neither the principle nor the sole concern of Christianity. For the primary purpose of God in the incarnation and the indwelling of the Spirit is sanctification, a purpose that is not contingent upon the occurrence of sin. This interpretation of Christianity actually undergirds and saves its gospel of redemption. For if God's chief end is the sanctification of all things, then the vanquishing of sin within history does not destroy the presupposition of Christology, but rather allows the purpose of God's presence with and in us to be fulfilled. A theology of sanctification, therefore, is not ambivalent with respect to the actual conquest of sin and weakness within history. It can fully and gladly use secular therapeutics. So it is not merely by chance that only American Christianity, the child of the Puritans and the radical reformation, has consistently affirmed and used psychotherapy, technology, social reform, and political action as adjuncts to the gospel. And it is not merely by chance that European Christianity still tends to interpret the increasing scientific control over the various therapeutic processes as a threat to God and to religion. In these two different attitudes toward the modern world the practical differences between a theology of sanctification and a theology of redemption are seen.

My argument in behalf of the assertion that the primary theme of Christian theology must be sanctification can also be developed with another issue in mind, viz., the problem of the *felix culpa*. To assert that the incarnation and the indwelling of the Spirit are chiefly for the sake of redemption is to make these two manifestations of the life of God totally dependent upon a mere contingency, namely, upon Adam's misuse of his freedom. But it seems intolerable that the great gifts of the incarnation and the indwelling of the Spirit—revelations of the innermost depths of God—should be dependent upon a contingent misuse of free choice by man, a "lucky fault."

To deal with the apparent disproportion between "the apple and the incarnation" some theologians upgrade the magnitude of sin to match the two great mysteries of divine life. Sin, these theologians tell us, is a mystery that originates in God's secret will, or in the nonbeing against which He must forever struggle, or in the rejection which illuminates election, or in some awesome darkness. Paul Tillich, Karl Barth, and certain of their younger followers perpetuate this new supralapsarian doctrine. By upgrading sin and evil into a cosmic (even divine) necessity, they also maintain the necessity of the incarnation whereby God struggles against sin and evil. Such an upgrading of evil would seem to be implied by every Christocentric theology—for whatever is necessary to the life of Jesus Christ must be regarded as ultimately necessary. There is an analogy here with the oddest of ancient heresies: that Judas is the greatest saint in the history of salvation because through his betrayal of Jesus Christ comes the redemption of the world. But this solution to the problem of evil is both immoral and illogical. It is immoral because it dignifies and justifies evil by making goodness and justice dependent upon it. It is illogical because it asserts that God seeks what He seeks by opposing what He seeks. For this reason, even the *felix culpa,* the admission that the incarnation is dependent upon the contingent misuse of freedom by Adam, is preferable to it. Far better that God's incarnation and indwelling be unnecessary than that evil be dignified for their sake.

However, the whole purpose of my essay has been to suggest that there is yet another alternative with respect to this problem. We can seek the reason for the incarnation of the Son and the indwelling of the Spirit in something other than man's need for redemption. We can seek the reason for these two acts in something essential to the life of God Himself rather than in some need of man, i.e., in sanctification rather than in redemption. We can seek their reason in that which God seeks for His own sake, namely, His holiness, the glory of God.

Epilogue

The ideas presented in this volume have been exploratory. Perhaps after revision and expansion certain of them can withstand criticism and provide a basis for further work. I have developed my arguments in relative independence of one another, not only because they deal with quite different problems, but also in the secret hope that if I must retract some, I will not have to sacrifice all. But in spite of the range of topics they cover, I believe that my several proposals corroborate and sustain one another. Eventually I hope to develop these and further proposals into a comprehensive theology, integrated by a sustained single argument. It might be of value, therefore, to conclude with comments on the more obvious interrelations among the ideas presented here.

(1) In the first essay, I argued that atheism is the beginning of all criticism because every intellectus has, as its principle, some characteristic conception of God. Moreover, I pointed out that cultures attempt to vindicate the truth of their intellectus by developing some typical proof for God's existence. Augustinian culture produced the ontological argument; late medieval culture, the cosmological argument; and modern culture, the moral argument. The emerging sociotechnic intellectus presupposes that ultimate reality is a unity through which all conflicts can be reconciled. It too must try to prove the truth of this conception through a typical argument for God's existence, viz., the henological. The argument which I have provided in the fourth essay, therefore, intends to fulfill this requirement.

(2) After characterizing the emerging sociotechnic intellectus in my

first essay, I have, in my second, attempted to show the specific meaning of sin and faith in this cultural context: sin is ideological conflict and faith is *fides reconcilians*. Some readers might be interested in comparing my argument with that of Norbert Wiener in *The Human Use of Human Beings*. Approaching the problem from another angle, Wiener argues that the ultimate threat to cybernetic society is "Manichaeanism," that attitude which supposes that reality is not one, but dual, and therefore affirms conflict as both necessary and good. The proper faith to oppose this threat to cybernetic society, argues Wiener, is "Augustinianism," i. e., the faith that all discord and lack of unity in the world is not a positive evil, but a mere confusion, or weakness, that lacks any *ontological* status. There is, therefore, a real agreement between Wiener's conclusions and my own. In my fourth essay, moreover, I have attempted to suggest the basic terms of a metaphysics of unity that excludes both dualism and nonbeing from ultimate reality. Some such metaphysics is required by a cybernetic view of the world.

(3) The second and final essays in this volume support, from different perspectives, a thoroughly volitional interpretation of sin. Sin is always the unjust act of a created free will; it is a contingent event. Moreover, even the idea of sin is unnecessary to the Christian understanding of God, since the incarnation and the indwelling of the Spirit do not presuppose it. As unjust acts, sin is always specific; it is always "sins." What is common to all sins is that they are cases of idolatry, for by choosing unjustly a man "worships himself," putting his own will above the will of God for him. In this way, a man makes himself his own idol by referring all things to himself for judgment. By calling sin "idolatry," therefore, we deny it is a "mystery" and call attention to the fact that it always manifests itself as specific finite threats to man's humanity. These finite threats are "problems" that can in principle be overcome. On the basis of this understanding, the Church should wholeheartedly affirm the use of all secular therapies. The positive judgment regarding secular therapies that is made throughout this volume presupposes both a moral conception of sin and an interpretation of Christianity as a religion of sanctification.

(4) To affirm the efficacy and value of secular therapies and technology, however, has created a crisis of belief for many Christians. This crisis has arisen not simply because Christians have traditionally conceived God in the sole function of Redeemer, but, more especially, because they have defined God in terms of some essence. They have

thought that God is God because He "knows" or "does" something
that no one else can know or do. (If anyone else could know or do
these things, then the ability to know or do them would not define God
alone.) Today, through technology, man's knowledge and power have
been so increased that he himself seems to have become "god" (under
the traditional definition). This is why some people claim that "God
is dead." My purpose in introducing the idea of "dignity," however, is
to suggest a new way to approach this problem. For if the distinguishing characteristic of God is a dignity rather than an essence ("holiness" rather than knowledge or power or eternity), then there can be
no conflict between the glory of God and sociotechnical knowledge.
The special analysis of "holiness" presented in the last essay is, therefore, essential to the earlier arguments in this volume.

(5) In the first essay, I have noted the crucial function that myths
and images play in guiding sociotechnical societies. In the third essay,
therefore, I have attempted a theoretical account of the capacity of
myths to perform this function. I have argued that myths are images in
which we have an affectional sense of the whole of reality; they are
"vague" ideas that encourage rational and empirical completion. Such
an explanation of myth seems adequate to account for the function
they must have in a sociotechnic world. Those readers who wish to
explore this problem further might begin with Kenneth Boulding's
The Image.

(6) Since the theory of myth I have presented excludes the possibility of demythologizing or reexpressing myths in purely ontological
concepts, the question might be raised whether this implies that myth
—not science or philosophy—finally determines our understanding of
the world. To affirm this conclusion, however, would not only be to
repudiate twenty-five hundred years of western thought, but also to
deny the possibility of what science has already accomplished (a contradiction in terms!). Hence, after reinstating myth and opposing the
demythologizers in my third essay, I have attempted in my fourth to
reinstate metaphysics and show the validity of science. For henological
metaphysics includes myth as one of its modes (i. e., as the knowledge
of wholes) and includes the empirical sciences as another. The effect
of reinstating metaphysics in this way is to demythologize *ontology*,
i. e., to resist the tendency to "image" reality in terms of any essence
or model by insisting that being is pure unity. Such a move, of course,
ties metaphysics directly to logic. From the above considerations, we

M

see that the arguments in the first, third, and fourth chapters of this volume are intended to corroborate one another.

(7) The sharp distinction between myth and science in my metaphysics is consistent with an interpretation of man's intellectual development as a process of differentiation. What may have been less obvious to the reader, however, is that this metaphysics is itself intended to be an example of such a differentiation. For it differs from classical henologies (e. g., Plotinus') by building on the modern differentiated notion of unity. In Greek mathematics, unity was conceived as the undifferentiated beginning of all else, the prime reality. From this point of view, the one is the whole since all else derives from it and expresses it. It transcends both the even ("2") and the odd ("3"); strictly speaking, it is not a number, but Number Itself. These notions are involved in Plotinus' henology.

It is hard for us today to realize the influence of this notion of unity on western thought. It provided the model of infinity and the starting point for all science and metaphysical thinking. It is only in relatively recent times that men have begun to realize that unity may be conceived not simply as the prime real number (as in "1, 2, 3, 4, 5 . . ."), but as a single term within a complex system of relations (as in "-3, -2, -1, 0, 1, 2, 3 . . .") and also as one unique individual among many unique individuals (as in "1, 10, 101, 1010, 10101 . . ."). In order for these new notions of unity to arise, the concept zero needed to be understood. In my henology, I have maintained the classical equation of being with unity, but have differentiated the modes of being in accordance with the three types of unity. It is with respect to these differentiations that my metaphysics differs from classical henologies; and with respect to these differentiations, it exemplifies my thesis about the character of man's intellectual development. Readers who are interested in examining an argument that resembles mine, though undertaken from the point of view of the history of mathematics, might study Tobias Dantzig's *Number, The Language of Science.*

Index